DATE DUE FOR RETURN

The loan period may be shortened if the item is requested.

A History of Egypt

Egypt occupies a central position in the Arab world. Its borders between sand and sea have existed for millennia and yet, for centuries, until 1952, the country was ruled by foreigners, remote from its neighbours. Afaf Lutfi Al-Sayyid Marsot's book explores the paradoxes of Egypt's history in a new edition of her successful *A Short History of Modern Egypt*. Charting the years from the Arab conquest, through the age of the mamluks, Egypt's incorporation into the Ottoman empire, the liberal experiment in constitutional government in the early twentieth century, followed by the Nasser and Sadat years, the new edition takes the story up to the present day. During the Mubarak era, Egyptians have seen major changes at home with the rise of globalization and its effects on their economy, the advent of new political parties, the entrenchment of Islamic fundamentalism and the consequent changing attitudes to women. The author explores these developments and what they have meant for the Egyptian people. This short history is ideal for students and for travellers visiting the region for the first time.

AFAF LUTFI AL-SAYYID MARSOT is Professor Emerita of History at the University of California at Los Angeles. Her previous publications include *Egypt in the Reign of Muhammad Ali* (1984) and *Women and Men in Late Eighteenth Century Egypt* (1995).

A History of Egypt

From the Arab Conquest to the Present

Second edition

AFAF LUTFI AL-SAYYID MARSOT
Professor of Near and Middle East History
University of California at Los Angeles

CAMBRIDGE
UNIVERSITY PRESS

CAMBRIDGE UNIVERSITY PRESS
Cambridge, New York, Melbourne, Madrid, Cape Town, Singapore, São Paulo

Cambridge University Press
The Edinburgh Building, Cambridge CB2 2RU, UK

Published in the United States of America by Cambridge University Press,
New York

ı OO5 324 O8S

www.cambridge.org
Information on this title: www.cambridge.org/9780521700764

First published 1985, thirteenth printing 2006, second edition 2007

Printed in the United Kingdom at the University Press, Cambridge

A catalogue record for this publication is available from the British Library

ISBN 978-0-521-87717-6 hardback
ISBN 978-0-521-70076-4 paperback

To my mother, Atiya Rashwan,
to V1 and V2 with all my love

Contents

Maps

Preface

The major theme of this book is the alienation of the population of Egypt from their rulers. Having suffered foreign occupations of various kinds, from the Arab conquest in 639 AD to the British occupation in 1882 which lasted until 1954, Egyptians through the ages have had to cope with alien rulers, or with rulers who were dominated by aliens so that a truly national government could be said to exist only after 1952. Yet throughout the eras of alien rule the native Egyptian recognized the existence of a fixed and unchanging territory that was Egypt, which had fixed natural boundaries, and which was separate as a territory even when it was the centre of an empire or amalgamated into an empire as a mere province. Thus the native Egyptian, while coping with alien rulers, also clung to the fixed piece of territory that he identified and knew as Egypt. Even before the age of nationalism made people conscious of national affinities Egyptians were conscious of living in a land called Egypt.

With the advent of the first native Egyptian government over fellow Egyptians after 1952 one would have expected the alienation of the rulers and the ruled to come to an end. Yet that alienation has persisted because the governments that came after 1952 were too insecure to adopt a truly representative government, and so opted for authoritarian and repressive rule which ended by representing vested interests rather than the interests of the majority such has been the characteristic of all successive governments. Even when political parties were allowed to exist, their freedom was restricted lest they vote for a change of ruler or of regime.

When Hosni Mubarak came to power after the death of Sadat he allowed political parties to reform and elections for parliament to take place. Yet the parties, save the major one supporting the regime are minority ones and often their members are proscribed, consequently the average Egyptian has not developed much faith in his parliamentary delegates, feeling that they are not truly representative. Furthermore the cabinet is not responsible to parliament but to the president. President Mubarak, had assured the public that he would not run for a fourth term, but a massive campaign was mounted in July 1999 to give him an oath of allegiance, a *baya*, a form of early Arab ceremony whereby people give their support to the person they wish as a leader. This was followed by an equally massive public relations attempt to present President Mubarak as the only viable candidate and he ran unopposed for another term, which he won in October 1999. Most of the population voted with its feet by staying away from the elections, in spite of government assurances that voter turnout was massive. Out of a population that is over seventy million, fifteen million allegedly voted positive. Banners congratulating the president on his victory were being painted two days before the voting had even begun. Throughout his term the president promised great changes, few of which were forthcoming. He also announced he would not stand for a fifth term but then changed his mind. His sole opponent Ayman Nour was eventually jailed and Mubarak won a fifth term of office. To date he has held power since 1981. Consequently it comes as no surprise to note that the Egyptian citizen feels nothing but cynicism towards his government allied by feelings of alienation.

I am grateful to Ms Hala Fattah for the care she took in reading the manuscript and helping with its index, and above all for her invaluable comments, which have greatly improved it. I am equally grateful to my husband Dr Alain Marsot for undertaking the same task, and for the patience and understanding with which he greeted the various revisions.

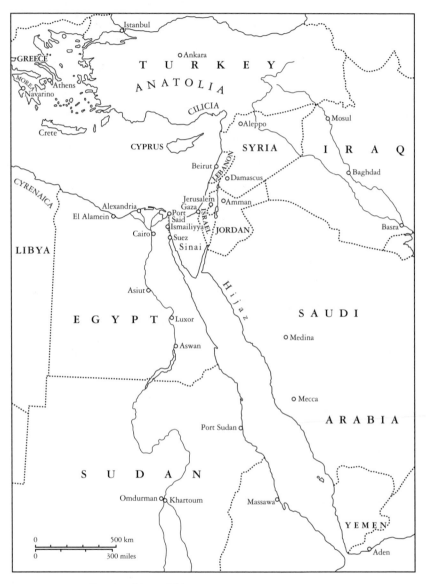

MAP I Egypt and its neighbours

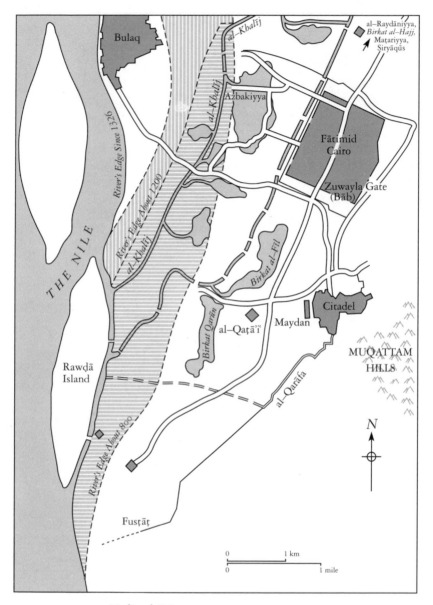

MAP 2 Medieval Cairo

I The Arab conquest of Egypt to the end of the Ayyubi dynasty, 639–1250

During the reign of Umar, the second caliph of the Arabs, Arab armies under the leadership of Amr ibn al-As invaded and conquered Egypt in 639 AD. Egypt was then a province of the Byzantine empire, ruled by a governor residing in Alexandria, the capital city. The inhabitants of Egypt, who were Monophysite Christians known as Copts, differed from the Melkite Christian Byzantines, who regarded monophysitical sects as heretical and treated them accordingly. The difference stemmed from disagreement over the nature of Christ. The Copts believed in his divine nature, while the Byzantines believed he was both human and divine. In consequence the Egyptians suffered from religious discrimination and persecution at the hands of their rulers, in addition to having to put up with a heavy burden of taxation to defray the expenses incurred through constant warfare between the Byzantines and their major rivals, the Sassanian empire. In brief, the population of Egypt resented the Byzantine domination of their country, and the burden of heresy that was laid upon them; they also resented the heavy taxation imposed upon them. Alienation of the population from their rulers was the hallmark of that period, as it was to be during successive periods due to differences in language, religion or ethnicity between rulers and ruled. Such alienation may not have mattered much to the population when government was efficient and administration just, but it was to become more important during periods of misrule and exploitation.

The Arab armies, numbering about eight thousand horsemen, found the conquest of Egypt an easy matter, for the native rulers cooperated with the new conquerors against their Byzantine overlords and helped open up the country to them. The Egyptians believed the Arabs would be more tolerant rulers than the Byzantines and would impose a lighter tax burden on them. The Greek presence in Egypt was then relatively weak as the empire was busy fighting the Arabs on other fronts, and had already lost its Syrian provinces to the Arabs in 636. The major battle between Arabs and Byzantines took place at Heliopolis and was decisive in opening the rest of Egypt to the Arabs. Rather than sacking the country and enslaving the population – a common practice in those days – the country was made to pay tribute and the prisoners were released, for the caliph Umar said, 'Tribute is better than booty; it lasts longer.'

The Egyptians were offered a choice between adopting Islam as their religion, or retaining their religion and paying a poll tax. When they opted for the latter, an agreement was drawn up between the Arab conquerors and the population which read: 'In the name of God, the merciful, the compassionate, this is the amnesty granted to the people of Egypt, to their religion, their goods, their churches and crosses, their lands and waters, nothing of which shall be touched or seized from them.' In return the Egyptians were expected to pay a land tax when the Nile waters reached a level that presaged a good harvest, that is when it reached 16 cubits; otherwise the taxes were remitted. The further obligation of offering three days' hospitality to Muslims was also imposed.

The Byzantine emperor repudiated the treaty between the Arabs and the Egyptians, but the local Coptic governor joined with Amr ibn al-As, the commander in chief of the Arab forces and the new governor of Egypt, against the Byzantines and in favour of the treaty. By 641 Byzantine attempts to recapture Egypt had failed and the whole of Egypt was incorporated within the expanding Arab empire. The majority of the population remained Christian and retained their own language, so that the process of Arabization and Islamization that eventually took place was to take several centuries. Egypt was now part of a large Arab Muslim empire. Gradually a new form of government and administration was imposed. The rulers of the country were aliens, speaking an alien language and worshipping an alien God, so that the alienation between rulers and ruled that characterized the Byzantine period was to be continued under the Arabs and their successors.

Amr, the new governor of Egypt, ruled justly and efficiently. Because the Arabs had conquered an empire with immense speed they had not had time to develop an administrative apparatus of their own, and so adopted the form of government they found in each territory they conquered. It was only towards the end of the century that a new form of administration came into existence. The Byzantine form of government, a system which divided the country into provinces each ruled by a provincial governor who reported to a central governor residing in Alexandria, continued with a few minor changes. By and large that system, with minor modifications, was to be used throughout the history of Egypt. The capital was moved from Alexandria to a more central location, and a new city, given the name Fustat (the Tent) and located a few miles south of present-day Cairo, was built as the new capital. The central area of the new town housed a mosque, named the mosque of Amr, which remains to the present day though much rebuilt and altered.

At first the Egyptians tended to look down on the less refined Arabs. Amr, a man of wit and discernment, allegedly decided to teach the Egyptians a lesson. He gave a three-day banquet, to which all were invited. On the first day he served camels as the main course, much to the disgust of the Egyptians who were accustomed to more delicate fare, but the Arabs fell to with hearty appetites. The next day he served the delicacies of Egypt, and his men wiped the boards clean with an equally voracious appetite. On the third day he had his soldiers parade in battle formation while he addressed the crowd: 'The first day's entertainment was to show you the plain food of the desert Arabs; the second was to show you that we can also appreciate the finer things in the conquered lands; the third day is to show you that we still retain our martial valour.' The lesson was not lost on the Egyptians. Caliph Umar approved Amr's finesse and commented that the art of warfare depended on wisdom as well as on the use of force.

No spoliation was permitted the army by Amr, so that little destruction or devastation was incurred. The tale that he ordered the famous library at Alexandria burned is fictitious, appearing six hundred years later. No land was confiscated from the Egyptians, and Caliph Umar stringently forbade any Arab to own land in Egypt, for fear that through vested interests he would lose his fighting forces to other territories. Umar was so adamant that when Amr asked whether he could build a house for himself, he was refused.

The governor of Egypt was appointed by the caliph in Mecca, but the governor appointed three chief officials of the province: the marshal, the chief judge (qadi) and the treasurer. The marshal controlled the army and the police; the qadi applied the law; the treasurer supervised the collection of taxes. Frequently the treasurer was nominated by the caliph, for apart from collecting taxes the treasurer's function also included remitting funds to the governor to defray the expenses of the province and sending the surplus to the imperial treasury abroad.

The majority of the taxes came from the poll tax which was applied to wage-earning males only and excluded women, children, the aged, priests and religious dignitaries of either the Christian or the Jewish sects. The land tax (the kharaj) was imposed on a million and a half acres which formed the total cultivable land at the time. The population was estimated at 6–8 million men, which would give a total population of some 20–30 million people. Land production was increased through a series of irrigation projects carried out by Amr, and it seems there was a central body of officials who supervised all irrigation. Though each province was responsible for the upkeep of its dykes, dams and canals, the entire irrigation system was centralized. Corvée labour, which pressganged men, was the means of maintaining, cleaning and repairing canals and dams, the lifeline of the irrigation system. Amr reopened the ancient canal that joined the Nile to the Red Sea and facilitated the transport of grain to the Hijaz. Egypt became the granary of the Arabs. The canal remained in use for eighty years, until neglect once again allowed it to become totally clogged up with sand.

The Egyptians were content under Amr's wise rule, but Caliph Umar died in 644 and was succeeded by Uthman, who chose to replace Amr by his half-brother Abdullah, who raised the taxes, increasing the revenue but placing a heavier burden on the people. When Uthman pointed out to Amr the greater sums remitted to the capital saying, 'the camel yields more milk', Amr retorted, 'Yes, but to the detriment of her young'. Disaffection was sown among the population as a result of Abdullah's stringent policies. The people revolted and refused to admit Abdullah into the country when he returned from a journey to Palestine. The fight over the political control of Egypt was carried to Mecca. Caliph Uthman was eventually assassinated by a contingent of Arabs, stationed in Egypt but led by one of the Meccan aristocracy, who came to complain of Abdullah's policies in Egypt, but who also sought a more equitable share of political appointments in the empire.

After the assassination of Uthman, Ali, the prophet's son-in-law and cousin, became the fourth caliph. Muawiya, Uthman's cousin and the governor of Syria, then demanded revenge for his cousin's death and was helped by Amr. Due to Amr's astuteness Muawiya's demand for revenge was soon promoted to a rival claim to the caliphate. When Muawiya eventually succeeded Ali as caliph (thus founding the Umayya dynasty of caliphs), he granted Amr the governorship of Egypt and all its revenues. The province was then said to be so rich that when Amr died at the age of ninety in 664 he left what historians tell us was 2 *ardabs*, or 396 lb, of gold. Historians also add that Amr's sons refused to inherit that gold, deeming it earned in sin.

After the death of Amr and over the following two centuries Egypt was ruled by ninety-eight governors in a system that alternated mild and generous rule with severity and religious oppression, depending on the character and the whim of the governor appointed, his relationship with the people, his economic needs, and those of the imperial treasury. Various Arab tribes were allowed to migrate into Egypt, where they settled and intermarried with the population, thus hastening the process of Arabization. The previous law laid down by

Umar, that no Arab could own property outside the Arabian peninsula, was infringed, and Arabs now came to own land in Egypt and
elsewhere in the newly conquered territories.

With the advent of the Umayya dynasty and especially during the
reign of Abd al-Malik ibn Marwan (685–705), the administration began
to change. The language of the public registers was changed to Arabic
from the previous Coptic, so that Copts, unless they learned Arabic,
were perforce replaced in the administration by Arabs. The change of
personnel was also accompanied by a change in coinage, which became
purely Islamic and was minted at the capital of the empire, now
Damascus. A regular postal service tied the provincial capitals more
closely to the imperial capital. These fiscal and administrative changes
were eventually to turn Coptic-speaking Christian Egypt into Arabic-
speaking Muslim Egypt, with a small Christian minority, the Copts,
who today form around ten per cent of the population. In time Coptic
as a language faded away to become a liturgical language known only
to priests and monks, although in the nineteenth century there was a
revival of that language, but not a very successful one.

The conflicts, both sectarian and political, that had rent the
Arabian peninsula, overthrowing caliphs and dynasties, found echoes
in Egypt, which became plagued by a series of insurrections arising
from conflicts between different groups of Muslim Arabs who had
settled in the country. These conflicts raged among the orthodox (or
Sunni) majority of Muslims, and those who followed the minority
sect, the followers of Ali (Shii). The latter believed that leadership of
the Muslims should go to Ali and to his descendants. On several occasions the Copts also rose in revolt to protest against oppressive taxation. Their uprisings were repressed with cruelty and severity, and
with each wave of repression some Copts would convert to Islam in
the hope of escaping future oppression. Others became Muslim in the
hope of avoiding paying the poll tax, but this did not help them, for
under the Umayya dynasty, except for a brief period of two years, they
were forced to pay taxes even when they had converted to Islam. Still
others converted for a variety of reasons common to all converts.

The policy followed by the Umayya dynasts was to avoid settling internal problems within the provinces of the empire, preferring the use of repression or of military expansion to divert attention from such problems. The root cause of conflict within the empire was thus never addressed and continued to fester. Conflict mostly resulted from unfair taxation and increased exploitation, especially when the Egyptian people had not identified with their Arab conquerors.

Under the Abbassi rulers (750–1258), who succeeded the Umayya, Egypt fared as badly, if not worse, for now ruthless and unscrupulous rulers abused the population and extorted monies from them illegally. The only protection the people now had against abuse of power was to appeal to the chief judge, the qadi. The qadi applied the law (the *sharia*) which was based on the Koran, the sayings of the prophet Muhammad and the customary practices of areas of the Arab empire. Four legal schools of jurisprudence eventually came to be recognized as having equal validity, although only three of them had any following in Egypt: the Shafii, the Maliki, and the Hanafi schools. The qadi protected the population from the rapacity of governors, for he determined whether a tax procedure was legal or not, and whether a new tax was permissible or not. Despite depredations on the part of the governors, the city of Fustat flourished and became a metropolis, a commercial and trading centre.

From 834 Egypt was granted in military tenure (an *iqta*) to members of the Turkish oligarchy which had seized power in Baghdad, then the Muslim capital of the Abbassi dynasty. The governors of Egypt thus changed from Arabs to Turkish military rulers, who were granted the province in tenure and therefore ruled it as though it were a personal possession rather than as a province that was part of an empire to be governed according to fixed and established rules. In one sense that personal form of government was to keep Egypt separate from the rest of the imperial provinces and to develop in it (some would say continue) some form of self-identity – a recognition of an Egyptian self – other than the greater identity belonging to a Muslim Arab empire. This is not to imply that Egyptians had developed a national identity at such an early stage, but it is to point out that they have always identified themselves, from Pharaonic times, as inhabitants of a fixed and unchanging entity known as Egypt. At times that entity was incorporated as a province within an empire; at others it became the centre of an empire. Throughout its political and administrative vicissitudes the country remained the same territorial entity bounded by its natural frontiers, the deserts on either side of the Nile, which had in the past protected it from invasions, and the Mediterranean Sea to the north. While an inhabitant of Egypt identified himself as an inhabitant of a village or town, as a member of a religious community, and as being of a specific ethnicity – native Egyptian or Egyptianized Arab – he also recognized the existence of a fixed territory called Egypt to which he belonged.

One of the early Turkish governors sent to rule Egypt by the Abbassi government in 868 was Ahmad ibn Tulun. A man of ability, education and intelligence, he rapidly grasped the potential of the country. Because of its natural frontiers and its distance from the imperial capital (perhaps he also knew the growing weakness of the Abbassis), he determined to make himself the ruler of an autonomous state and even to expand his frontiers along the trade routes and conquer neighbouring territories. Thus ibn Tulun was the first in a series of rulers who were to turn Egypt *de facto* into an independent state ruled briefly by one opportunist governor after another supposedly subservient to the Abbassis, but to all intents and purposes independent of them, except for the mention of the caliph's name during the Friday prayers and the sending of a small sum as tribute. Mention of the caliph's name on Fridays and the minting of coins were the two prerogatives of kingship recognized at the time.

Once he had made sure of his absolute authority in Egypt, Tulun built a new capital city for himself. This was a city north of Fustat, which he named al-Qatai (the Wards) because each ethnic group in his army and each division among his retainers was settled in a separate quarter that was assigned to that specific group. The city was one square mile in size. It contained a palace surrounded by a vast garden and another palace to house the ladies of the harem. A hippo-drome, stables and a menagerie for wild animals which the ruler fancied, were also set up. A mosque, vast enough to contain the entire army within its precincts, was designed and built by a Coptic architect. The mosque, which still stands to the present day and is still used for prayers, is architecturally interesting for its use of brick as a building material, instead of the more common stone, and for its pointed arches which one historian describes as antedating similar arches in England by two hundred years. The gesso work on the arches and the coloured glass windows are remarkably beautiful. The outer wall of the mosque was surrounded by shops of various kinds. Business was said to be so flourishing then that the shops changed hands three times a day, going to different sellers, who could make enough money working for one-third of the day to satisfy their needs. Tulun carried out other public works, such as an aqueduct for bringing water from the Nile up to the palace and repairing the Nilometer, the gauge which measured the height of the Nile flood at the island of Roda.

A generous man, Tulun daily distributed alms to the poor and kept an open house, feeding any, of whatever estate, who came to his table. He was said to have spent nearly half a million dinars (the gold coin of the day) on building his new city, and soon had need for funds to support his various charities, his building programme and his army. He then diminished the sum remitted to the imperial capital as tribute, and when he later came into conflict with the caliph he cut out the tribute altogether. The revenue of Egypt was said to come to only 4,300,000 dinars a year, so that Tulun probably found other means for increasing his funds than the income from the territory itself. He forced the religious dignitaries who controlled vast estates to lend money, but he soon turned his thoughts to expanding his frontier in the direction of Syria, that is, along the major trade route into the country. Control of Syria was a sure means of enriching the treasury but it also brought him into conflict with the caliph, who sent an army against his vassal. The army never came close to the Egyptian borders and was forced to withdraw for lack of funds with which to carry out the intended campaign. Another campaign along the Mediterranean littoral extended his dominion up to Barka. It was after the conquest of Syria that Tulun minted coins bearing his own name as well as the name of the Abbassi caliph. He also tried to extend his frontiers in the direction of Mecca but his forces were repelled and he was cursed from the pulpits for his heinous deed in attacking a holy city.

Under the benevolent rule of ibn Tulun the country prospered; agriculture and commerce flourished, for the ruler carefully supervised administration and saw to it that his tax collectors dealt fairly with the people. Peculation, which had been practised by the treasurers sent by the Abbassis, was strictly prevented. Taxes thus fell instead of rising as more new sources of wealth were tapped. The ruler's riches did not come at the expense of the population; rather the population shared in the new wealth. Tulun's generosity became proverbial, for he never turned away anyone who applied to him for assistance. He was however a hasty man who sometimes sentenced men of his entourage to death, but such actions did not affect the native population, which was content and quiescent under his rule.

When Tulun died he left a treasure of ten million dinars, a fleet of one hundred ships, which gives us an inkling of the extent of his commercial wealth, and a stud of three hundred horses, as well as thousands of donkeys, mules and camels. He was succeeded by his second son, Khamarawaih, so that the government of Egypt became transformed into a dynasty of rulers. Tulun's oldest son, for he had seventeen sons, had risen in revolt against his father when the father was fighting in Syria, and had in consequence been imprisoned for life. Good government however died with ibn Tulun, for his successors were profligate, incompetent bunglers, who fought each other over the succession and depleted the treasury. This was particularly evident after the death of Khamarawaih. Relations between the Tuluni ruler and the Abbassi caliph were strained even after Khamarawaih's daughter, Qatr al-Nada (Dewdrop), was married to the caliph. The accounts given of the lady's wedding preparations boggle the mind and read like a tale out of the Arabian Nights, for her father had palaces erected along the entire route, so that his daughter should sleep every night in a palace until she had arrived in Baghdad. The last Tuluni ruler was eventually defeated by the caliph's armies, which sacked and ruined the city of al-Qatai leaving nothing standing but the mosque. The population of the country was treated like a conquered people by the invaders while plunder and extortion brought low a state that had so recently enjoyed an unprecedented degree of wealth and prosperity.

For the next thirty years government of Egypt at the hands of Turkish governors and their wilful and undisciplined armies was a mockery. The soldiers who came with the governors dictated their terms to their leaders, and the governors, forced to rely on the soldiers in order to maintain their rule in an alien country, extorted funds from the population to keep the army happy and contented. The hold of these governors on the land was precarious at best, and they were frequently beset by armies invading the country from North Africa. The treasurers who were sent from the imperial capital were corrupt and robbed the country, while the soldiers who were supposed to guard and protect the country, more frequently plundered and looted at will.

Eventually a period of good government came to the land when Muhammad ibn Tughg al-Ikhshid was sent as governor in 935. His firm hand brought order out of chaos and no disturbances occurred in eleven years. Al-Ikhshid had been governor of Damascus before being appointed to Egypt. He had brought his army with him and so was able to dominate the situation, bringing about a welcome period of peace and prosperity. Al-Ikhshid and his heirs were also governors of Syria and of the holy cities of Mecca and Medina for a period of thirty years. After that time the authority of the Abbassi caliphs was greatly weakened; they were subject to their praetorian guards, who deposed, maimed and blinded caliphs at will. Real power remained in the hands of the military oligarchy. The empire by then was breaking up into petty principalities as each provincial ruler set up a dynasty in his province. Al-Ikhshid had given shelter to a caliph who was fleeing his guards and who rewarded him by making his government over Egypt hereditary, but the caliph returned to his capital to meet death at the hands of his guards. Al-Ikhshid and his heirs remained in control of Egypt, although each new ruler in the dynasty sought a formal ratification from the caliph for his rule, as Egypt remained an Abbassi province in spite of the fact that the Abbassis had little or no influence over it.

Historians of these early periods tell us little about the common people; they merely recount whether government was oppressive or not, the country prosperous or not. We do however have accounts of national festivals, some of which are still held today. One such festival commemorates the rise of the Nile waters in the summer months when dams are broken in mid-September to allow the flood free circulation. The parched land is flooded with silt and water, and hope springs anew that the crops will be rich, and prosperity reign. That used to happen only if the Nile reached a height of 16 cubits, as measured by the Nilometer. Were the waters too high or too low the spectre of famine hovered over the land, for the land was either parched or flooded and in both cases the crops were ruined. Once the waters receded in January the dams were rebuilt, crops sown and later harvested. A system of dams and canals allowed some of the Nile water to be stored, and strips of land bordering the Nile could grow a second crop through irrigation by such devices as the water wheel *(saqiya)* or the Archimedean screw *(shaduf)*, which lifted the waters in the canals and poured them onto the soil. Egypt was predominantly an agricultural country and remained so until well into the middle of the last century.

From ancient Egyptian times the rise of the Nile waters has been greeted as a festive occasion by the Egyptians. In ancient days it was said that a Nile bride was thrown alive into the river to symbolize the marriage of the earth with the waters. When Egypt converted to Christianity the feast was celebrated as the epiphany and renamed the 'Feast of Immersion' in memory of the baptism of Christ. Under the Muslims the same feast continued to be celebrated as a sign of God's grace that the river faithfully and continuously brought its bounty every year.

During the festival the banks of the Nile as well as the entire city were illuminated with multicoloured lamps or torches. The population gathered on the banks of the river, or sailed on the river in boats twinkling with lights. Dressed in their holiday best, people picnicked on the banks of the river, played music, sang and danced in celebration of the flood. There was a popular belief that on that one night a swim in the river would preserve the bather from disease.

For twenty-two years, from 947 until the end of the Ikhshidi dynasty, Egypt was governed by a black eunuch named Abu al-Misk Kafur (Musky Camphor), who was tutor to al-Ikhshid's sons. The country was rent by a series of natural disasters. Terrible earthquakes were followed by a great fire that was said to have destroyed 1,700 houses in Fustat. Successive low Nile floods brought famine and want, and an invasion from the south laid low Upper Egypt and devastated its crops. In the midst of these calamities Kafur maintained a splendid court which gathered poets and artists, among whom was the most brilliant Arab poet of his time, al-Mutanabbi. At first al-Mutanabbi, when invited to Egypt and showered with largesse, had written panegyrics in praise of his new and generous patron, but he soon found himself a virtual captive who was not allowed to leave the court or the country. In time he managed to escape and penned the most bitter and brilliant satire against his erstwhile host. For a while Kafur was adulated by the poets, one of whom attributed the earthquakes that ravaged the country to the earth shaking with joy at the blessing of such a ruler as Kafur. Kafur enjoyed even tongue-in-cheek praise and kept a firm hand on the reins of government. He beautified the capital with new buildings and carried out public works to turn his capital into a centre of culture and civilization.

The inhabitants of the city benefited from the trade and commerce that flowed through the urban centres, but the majority of the population, the rural inhabitants, paid the high taxes that supported the life of luxury of their overlords. By the tenth century the majority of the inhabitants of Egypt had converted to Islam, and had intermarried with Arabs who migrated in waves to settle in that rich and fertile land.

The year of Kafur's death, 968, was the beginning of the end for the dynasty. The rising power of the Fatimi dynasty of North Africa was inevitably attracted to the idea of conquering a country that was ill-managed and ill-protected. In 969 the Fatimi army invaded Egypt and reached Fustat.

Al-Muizz li Din Allah al-Fatimi, who claimed descent from the Prophet through his daughter Fatima and the Prophet's cousin Ali, was the fourth caliph of the North African kingdom. The schisms that had rent the Muslim empire into Sunni and Shii factions had given birth to an offshoot of Shii Islam known as the Ismaili (or Seveners). An Ismaili missionary had made his way from Baghdad to North Africa and rapidly acquired a following among the local population. He succeeded in rousing the people to eject their last Aghlabi ruler and proclaim the birth of a new kingdom led by a descendant of the Prophet. Thus was born Fatimi rule in North Africa. Whether the new ruler was a descendant of the Prophet or not was really of no consequence to any save the men of religion. Though these were not able to come to any kind of consensus about the lineage of the new rulers, the Fatimi created an empire which ran from Fès in modern-day Morocco to the frontiers of Egypt, and their followers accepted their claims of prophetic descent.

On several prior occasions the Fatimi armies had invaded and briefly occupied Egypt, only to be driven out. During the three decades of Ikhshidi rule the Fatimis had not attempted to invade Egypt, but the last days of Kafur's rule clearly revealed the inherent weaknesses of the state and the lack of efficient successors, and opened the way for what became an easy conquest of Egypt, the only one, until modern days, to come from the west. The only prior western invasion had occurred during pharaonic days.

Al-Muizz was a highly educated man who was also a born statesman and a wise and generous ruler. He carefully laid his plans for the invasion of Egypt which had been attempted by his predecessors without success. Wells were dug along the route to Egypt, treasure collected and payment lavished on the army to prevent any disgruntled soldiery from sabotaging the campaign. One hundred thousand men were sent to invade Egypt under the generalship of a freed man, Jawhar the Sicilian (al-Siqilli). The invading army was aided by a series of natural catastrophes in Egypt. A terrible famine had broken out in 967, followed by a plague which reportedly killed some half a million people in the capital. Furthermore the death of Kafur had left Egypt in chaos. On 1 July 969, the Fatimi army entered the Egyptian capital.

Jawhar immediately set about building a fortified city, a new capital for his master. The new city was square, each side being less than a mile in length. Maghrabi astrologers consulted the stars, waiting for an auspicious omen before digging the foundations. Ropes marked the periphery of the new structures and bells were hung on the ropes to give a signal for the workers to begin digging. The legend goes that a raven landed on the ropes which set the bells ringing and the workers digging before the horrified astrologers could stop them. Since it was too late to stop the workers, the astrologers went back to their books to see what star or planet was in the ascendancy at that time; they found the planet Mars, al-Qahir in Arabic, so the new city was named al-Qahira, otherwise known to the non-Arabic-speaking world as Cairo.

Judiciously al-Muizz had sent shipments of grain to alleviate the famine in Egypt and thus win the favour of the starving people. Merchants found hoarding grain were flogged and forced to sell to the population at a reasonable price. The plague lasted for two years and it was only in 971–2 that a good Nile flood finally gave promise of a decent harvest. Mysteriously the plague disappeared. Jawhar ruled wisely and well until his lord arrived. He had a new mosque built in 970, known as the mosque of al-Zahra, after Fatima al-Zahra, the prophet's daughter. Public works on mosque and palace supplied employment to artisans and artists and alleviated the straitened conditions of the city.

The population of Egypt accepted without protest the rule of a Shii, even though they were Sunni, for his rule brought plenty and security. Moreover the Fatimis did not try to impose their beliefs on the population. Soon the holy cities, Mecca and Medina, accepted the suzerainty of Muizz, as did northern Syria and, after a series of battles, the rest of Syria. Once again Egypt became the centre of a mighty empire that spanned two continents, but an empire which, though rich and powerful, was ruled by people espousing a different form of Islam from that of the common people. While normally the differences of religious belief did not affect everyday life, these differences were highlighted by a Fatimi ruler who imposed extraordinary laws on the population and by the presence of foreign soldiers. Having grown accustomed to one set of soldiers – Arabs and Turks – Egyptians now had to become used to another set – Berbers, and (later) blacks from the Sudan. The segment of the population that most keenly felt its isolation from the rest of the Sunni world was the segment of the men dealing with religious matters, the *ulama*. Intellectually and doctrinally they were isolated from mainstream thought for the two centuries that Fatimi rule lasted in Egypt. That isolation was to allow them to develop along lines of their own and to acquire thought processes that differed from those of mainstream Muslims. Not only were they isolated from Sunni thought but they were also faced with Ismaili ulama and, while no constraints were put upon them, nevertheless they had to counter a different interpretation of their religious beliefs and a different intellectual tradition.

In 973 Muizz finally arrived in his new territory. During the first audience he gave, the learned men of Egypt gathered to meet him and asked him to present them with his credentials and his genealogy before they could accept him without reservation as a descendant of the Prophet. Many of the ulama were themselves descended from the Prophet, *ashraf*, as they were called. The story is related that when that request was put to Muizz he drew his sword and said, 'There is my genealogy.' Then he showered the floor with gold coins and said: 'There is my lineage.' The ashraf had nothing further to say. The story, probably apocryphal, exemplified Fatimi rule in Egypt – rule by force of arms, but also a rule that would be benevolent and financially rewarding.

The new capital, which was really a fortified palace-cum-barracks for the invading army, was placed out of bounds to the Egyptians after sundown. Equally the city of Fustat was out of bounds to the soldiers once the sun had set, to prevent any friction between civilians and soldiers. Qahira was the residence of the new caliph, his family, servants and retainers, who were said to number eighteen thousand. Within the enclosure stood a smaller palace across from the great palace, and between them lay a hippodrome where ten thousand troops could parade at the same time. The palaces were connected by underground passageways. Historians have given us accounts of the lavish manner in which the palaces were furnished. This was an era of artistic flowering, the high Middle Ages, and one of wealth as a consequence of expanding international trade with the East and with Europe, as well as good government.

Muizz had brought with him a great fleet. Soon Egyptian harbours were expanded; a dock was built at Maks – later replaced by Bulaq when alluvium from the Nile widened the distance between Maks and the river – as the northern river port of Cairo. Misr, the name given to the agglomeration of buildings which formed the old Byzantine city, was the southern river port for the capital. Both river ports had arsenals and shipyards, and both had docks where customs duties were gathered before goods were allowed to leave the ports.

The new ruler was interested in all matters of administration, thereby earning the esteem of his new subjects. Perhaps his most appreciated action was to disband the previous system of tax-farmers and tax-collectors that had preyed upon the population during the days of the Ikhshidis, and to appoint new officers to estimate and fix tithes and land taxes, and to examine any complaints made by the people regarding unjust or excessive taxation. Revenue increased even when taxes were strictly collected, because the collectors no longer pocketed the taxes and were fair in their estimations. By then the centre for Islamic trade and commerce had clearly shifted from Baghdad to Cairo.

Fatimi rule was to last in Egypt for two centuries until 1171. Some of the rulers and their viziers (ministers) were rapacious and heedless of the welfare of their subjects; others righted the balance. The Fatimi army, which on first arriving in Egypt had been a homogeneous grouping of Berber tribesmen and which prided itself on its strict sense of discipline, soon lost both its homogeneity and its discipline when Turkish mercenaries and Sudanese troops from the south were added. These different ethnic factions soon became a bane to the ruler and to his hapless population with their internecine fighting and savage depredations.

Muizz's son Aziz succeeded his father to the throne and, while he was a wise ruler who gave his administrators fixed salaries to end any corruption, he was also the one who imported the Turkish troops. On the other hand Aziz's son, al-Hakim Bi-Amr Allah (the One Who Reigns by the order of God), was an enigma, if not an eccentric. Under his rule strange laws were passed. For example, shoemakers were forbidden to make shoes for women, who were enjoined not to leave their houses and not to be seen in public. *Mulukhiyya* (Jew's mallow), a favourite food among Egyptians, was banned because Muawiya, the founder of the Umayya caliphate, who had caused the downfall of the Prophet's son-in-law, loved it. Games were forbidden. Beer and wine were poured into the Nile, along with honey.

For the first decade of Hakim's rule minorities enjoyed privileges. Then they were persecuted, so that many were said to have converted to Islam during that period to escape persecution. Yet the caliph's leading advisers were Christians. Whether Christian or Muslim, many viziers were executed, and a special department was set up for the confiscation of property of disgraced public officials.

Among Hakim's positive acts was the foundation in 1005 of a centre of learning called the House of Wisdom (Bait al-Hikma).

Although aimed at propagating Shii learning, the Bait had an enormous library of books and was open to anyone who wished to study sciences, law, theology, etc., whether the student followed Shii or Sunni sects.

One of Hakim's viziers was a man named Darazi, who expounded the belief that Hakim was the incarnation of the godhead. The citizens of the capital, who had put up with a great deal in past years, found such beliefs intolerable. It was not only that the idea was heretical to Muslims, but also that, having suffered many years of economic hardship under Hakim and put up with his eccentric laws, the people felt that this was the last straw. Furthermore the citizens, who were apt to make fun of everything and everyone, were amused at their ruler's interdiction on the appearance of women in public thoroughfares and hung the effigy of a woman in the city of Fustat. Hakim was so enraged by the effigy that he sent his black troops to burn down the city, which was done. Darazi's theory also shocked the Turkish troops, who besieged the palace along with the population and howled for Darazi's head. Hakim smuggled Darazi out of the palace and out of Egypt, while coolly facing his citizens and assuring them that Darazi was not in the palace. Darazi fled to Lebanon where he founded the Druze sect in the mountains.

Once again Hakim sent his black troops to burn and ravage Fustat in punishment for the insolence of its citizens in questioning his wisdom and that of his vizier. After a period of persecution of both Muslims and Christians, Hakim suddenly rescinded all his previous rules for Muslims, claiming that such laws had been of a purely allegorical nature. He also rescinded the discriminatory practices against Christians. But by then the Berber troops in the army had joined forces with the Turkish troops against the black regiments, whose power, in consequence, was broken by the new alliance. The black troops, who in the past had been ready to obey Hakim's orders, now found themselves at the mercy of the other regiments and there was little Hakim could do about it.

On 13 February 1021 Hakim, who was accustomed to wander alone in the hills around Cairo and meditate, disappeared. His body was never found, and the Druze believe that one day he will reappear to reveal truth and usher in the day of judgement. The rest of the population believed various stories about the disappearance; most of them claimed that Hakim's sister had had her brother assassinated in order to seize power.

Hakim's successors were incompetent and unable to control the army and its various ethnic groups. Years of famine came to make the internal situation worse. Famine and revolt together lasted for six years until 1027, when a good Nile flood brought relief to the country and a plentiful harvest that ended the famine.

The Fatimi empire did not retain control over all its territories for long: its area was too extensive and posed problems of logistics. The North African territories could not for long be controlled by absentee rulers and they threw off Ismailism, returned to the Sunni fold and acquired local rulers. Syria was to fall to the Buwaihis, a military oligarchy that dominated the Abbassi caliphs, and then to the Seljuks who replaced the Buwaihis as oligarchs. These last set up city states in the region of Syria and northern Iraq. By 1071 Sicily, too, was wrested from the Fatimis, when it was conquered by the Normans. In spite of these losses Egypt continued to prosper for a long time, for trade and commerce flourished.

A Persian traveller named Nasiri Khusrau, who visited Cairo from 1046 to 1049, left us an interesting description of both Cairo and Fustat. He described them both carefully, which was valuable to posterity since the original cities, especially Fustat, were eventually completely ruined. He wrote that Cairo was a city of some twenty thousand houses all built of brick, but so carefully was the brick joined that it looked as though the houses had been constructed of stone. The houses were five and six storeys high and were surrounded by gardens and orchards irrigated by wells. The shops of the city, also estimated at twenty thousand, were the property of the ruler and represented an annual income of about one and a quarter million dinars.

The city of Fustat, a mile from Cairo, was built on an elevation so that to the Persian it seemed as though the houses were of seven to fourteen storeys. He claimed that some of the buildings were capable of housing 350 people each. Some of the streets were covered and all were lit with lamps. The markets amazed him with the sumptuous goods they contained: pottery so delicate it was translucent; metallic lustre ware (for which the city was famous), which imitated metal and yet was only glazed to look like metal, thereby enabling Muslims to obey the religious injunction not to eat out of silver and gold vessels; exquisite, transparent, green glass. The shops of the jewellers and the money changers were untended, yet no one stole anything and shopkeepers sold at a fixed price. Anyone found cheating the customers was paraded in a public ceremony of humiliation. Modern-day excavations – for nothing of Fustat remains above ground – have confirmed much of Khusrau's description. They have uncovered an efficient and elaborate sewage system which must have contributed to the cleanliness and healthy atmosphere of the city. The sewers ran underground and were deep enough for a man to walk upright in. They were serviced every day through kiosks dotted along the sewer lines, where lime could be poured in.

Khusrau's description of Cairo was made during the reign of the caliph al-Mustansir, who ruled longer than any other Muslim ruler, sixty lunar years, from 1036 to 1094. One of his viziers discovered that the revenue from land tax was only one million dinars, compared to the more than four million that had been extracted from the population under ibn Tulun in the ninth century, and attempted to reform agricultural practices in order to impose higher taxes. He stopped merchants from buying up crops before they were harvested, a custom which ruined cultivators, who were thus paid lower prices for their harvest than they would have obtained on the open market after the harvest. The vizier also set up stores of corn as reserves in case of famine.

Though a careless ruler who left affairs of state in the hands of his viziers, al-Mustansir was generous, and his pension list was said to include 100,000 to 200,000 names every year. A loose hand on the reins of government, combined with the presence of a variety of ethnic groupings among the regiments, ended in bloody fights among the troops, who were soon to decimate the country. The black regiments controlled Upper Egypt, while the Turkish regiments controlled the capital and used their power to despoil the treasury and strip the palace of its sumptuous treasures.

A terrible famine coupled with a low Nile in 1065 ushered in seven years of dreadful want. Famines so severe that people allegedly resorted to cannibalism were followed by years of plague in a well-established pattern of misery that was to repeat itself on later occasions. Entire households died within twenty-four hours. The enormous wealth that al-Mustansir had accumulated, or inherited, after years of rule was totally dissipated by the soldiers who looted the palace and forced their caliph to sell his treasures in order to give them money. The library of 100,000 volumes that had been the pride of various Fatimi rulers was dispersed. Rare manuscripts were used by the Turkish soldiers to heat their bath fires, and the bindings used to mend their shoes. Yet a century later Saladin, on coming to Cairo, found a library of 120,000 tomes, which said much for the intellectual interests of Fatimi rulers.

Some of the treasures that were looted from the palace were described by historians: we hear of 10 lb of emeralds, 250 lb of pearls, golden mattresses, objets d'art of gold, silver, rock crystal, ebony and ivory, a turban encrusted with jewels which weighed 17 lb. The palace was emptied of its furnishings by the soldiers so the caliph could find no item of furniture to sit on and had to use a straw mat. In desperation at his rampaging army, the caliph sent for the governor of Acre, Badr al-Jamali, an Armenian slave who had risen to high office through his talents. In answer to the caliph's appeal al-Jamali arrived with his Syrian troops, subdued the mutinous regiments, restored the caliph's authority and instituted a just and benevolent government. Once again peace and prosperity returned to Egypt. Al-Jamali called upon builders to come to Cairo and his architects designed the thick walls and buttressed gates which still surround Fatimi Cairo.

Under the Fatimis the *fallahin* (peasants) were by and large well treated, although the upheavals occasioned by the regiments' infighting had repercussions over the entire population. The administration was stratified and the management of local affairs entrusted to local administrators; this was especially the case with the upkeep of dykes and canals. Tax burdens were light and the population contented. The Copts were entrusted with financial offices, which they retained to modern times, and the caliphs frequently donated funds for the upkeep of monasteries. Periods of oppression as under al-Hakim were rare. Although historians describe discriminatory practices applied to Christians, such as the wearing of black or the riding of donkeys instead of horses, by and large this was a good period of government. But that was soon to change with the advent of the Crusades.

The first Crusade had begun its march into Muslim territory and captured Jerusalem by 1099. Had that march happened a few decades earlier it would have been stopped by the military power of the Seljuks; had it happened a few decades later the might of the *mamluks* would have stopped it. The Crusades came when there was a power vacuum in the region. At first the Egyptian viziers welcomed the Christians, thinking they could use them as allies against the Seljuks, but when the Crusaders massacred seventy thousand defenceless Muslims who had surrendered in Jerusalem, and attacked the Egyptians in spite of a flag of truce, all illusions vanished.

Engagements between Crusaders and Fatimi armies occurred and Egypt was invaded in 1117. From then on the Fatimis spent their energies in repelling invasions. This was made difficult by factional struggles which once again broke out within the army and among rival viziers. The streets became so unsafe because of rioting soldiers that people lived in constant terror. Caliphs were massacred by viziers, who massacred each other with equal fervour. The women of the harem became so desperate that they cut off their long tresses and sent them to the governor of a province in Upper Egypt. This was the ultimate gesture of despair and a sign begging the man to come to their rescue. The governor, al-Salih Talai ibn Ruzaiq, responded to their plea and came to Cairo to re-establish law and order.

Meanwhile, in northern Syria, Nur al-Din Zanji had established his power and annexed Damascus in 1154. This rendered the kingdom of Jerusalem vulnerable and insecure. Zanji was a strict Sunni and could not bring himself to ally with the Ismaili Fatimis, but neither would he allow Egypt, a Muslim country, to fall under the yoke of the Crusaders. Egypt then became the scene of diplomatic activity, when both Zanji and the Crusaders courted it. Ruzaiq, the strong man in power, had been murdered and once again rivalry between viziers left the country vulnerable. Rival viziers allied themselves, one to Zanji and one to the Crusaders. On three occasions the armies of these two states invaded Egypt; on the last occasion in 1169 the Syrians of Zanji came to Egypt as allies to oust the Crusaders. During that campaign the city of Fustat was set on fire by the vizier as part of a scorched-earth policy to make it of little use to the Crusaders, and for fifty-four days the city was said to have burned with twenty thousand barrels of naphtha. Recently historians, basing themselves on archaeological research, have questioned the extent of the damage the conflagration caused to Fustat that earlier historians have claimed.

The Syrian troops who had come to Egypt were now in charge of defence and their leader was appointed vizier by the Fatimi caliph. When that leader died he was succeeded as vizier by his nephew, the famous Salah al-Din al-Ayyubi, known to the West as Saladin.

The anomaly of a Shii ruler, ruling through a Sunni vizier, who was also lieutenant to a Sunni ruler, was not lost on Saladin, a fervent Sunni, who determined to bring the Fatimi dynasty to an end. In the meantime prayers on Friday were recited in the names of both the Fatimi caliph and the Syrian ruler. The mention of the name of the ruler during the Friday prayers is one of the signs of kingship in Muslim lands.

Saladin's reputation among the Egyptians was enhanced by a series of skirmishes with Crusaders which ended in victory. The

Egyptians, who had not followed the Ismaili sect of their rulers, had remained firmly Sunni in their beliefs and probably welcomed a Sunni vizier in place of an Ismaili. To re-educate the Egyptians in the path of orthodoxy, Saladin founded three schools in 1170, the famous *madrasas* which were to expand and turn Egypt into a centre of intellectual life once again. The following year the name of the Abbassi caliph was proclaimed during the Friday prayers and the name of the Fatimi caliph simply dropped. By then the caliph lay dying and never even knew that he had been deposed by his new vizier.

Thus the Fatimi dynasty, which had lasted for two centuries, ended in 1171 with barely a whimper. It had witnessed periods of immense wealth and equally immense misery, but it had erected a number of monuments and produced objets d'art that identified that period as one of affluence and of exquisite taste. The population had borne the generally light hand of their Ismaili rulers, for the rulers had not tried to convert them. But intellectually the Shii scholars had been shunned by their Sunni counterparts, who had felt their isolation from their Arab Sunni colleagues. This was all to change under the rule of Saladin and his Ayyubi dynasty, which ushered in a more consistently glorious era. Egypt once more became the centre of a Sunni Muslim empire. Though prayers had been offered in the name of the Abbassi caliph, the caliphate was held at arm's length by the Ayyubis, who developed an autonomous empire of their own. Pride in self and in religion was the hallmark of the rulers, and the ruled could identify with them as heroes of Islam, even though ethnically they were Kurdish and Turkish.

For the first few years of his rule Saladin set out to consolidate his position in Egypt against further Crusader attacks and against internal enemies from among former Fatimi elements in the country. Once Zanji had died, leaving behind him a young son, Saladin no longer feared any other Muslim ruler and began a phase of expansion into Syria and wars against the Crusaders aimed at liberating the Holy Land.

In Cairo Saladin neglected the ostentatious palaces built by Fatimi rulers, which soon fell into ruin. He built himself a citadel on a hill overlooking the city, which one can still see standing today. From that vantage point he could dominate the entire city and never be as easily besieged as in the city on flat ground. An aqueduct supplied the city and the citadel with drinking water from the Nile. Most of Saladin's time was spent campaigning, so that little time was spent in Egypt. Those who ruled over Egypt in his name were his brother, Safadin, known as al-Malik al-Adil, and his vizier, al-Fadil, as well as a eunuch, Qaraqush, who supervised much of the public works carried out in the country. Qaraqush was so strict a taskmaster that his name has come down in modern parlance as an adjective describing any form of rule that is rigid and strict. In one sense it was fortunate for Egypt that Saladin spent most of his time abroad, since he had no financial sense, while his brother and his vizier both did, and kept a watchful eye on expenses in Egypt. A multitude of public works were carried out under the supervision of both these men, including a canal in Upper Egypt which is known as Bahr Yusif, after Saladin's second name (Salah al-Din Yusif), even though it had originally been dug by the Pharaohs and had silted up.

Externally events were favourable to Saladin's plans. Not only was Syria left with a young king, but Jerusalem was also left with a baby king who was a leper, and with problems of succession. Saladin, whose overriding concern was to free Muslim countries of the Crusaders, planned to unify the Muslim world under his rule and thus drive out the invaders. First he conquered Syria, then he caused all the rulers of Cilicia, Mosul and other Muslim lands to sign a truce swearing to keep peace among themselves. Later he conquered Iraq so that there were no longer any enemies on his flanks and he could turn his attention to the Crusaders. In 1179 he won a great victory over them at Marj Uyun.

Saladin was aware that the Crusaders were as much an economic danger as a religious one. He thus tried to change the direction of free trade in the Mediterranean in a bid to arrest the power of the Crusaders. He supported the rise of the spice merchants (the *karimi*), who are first heard of in the eleventh century. Excluding all Christian merchants from trade in the Red Sea, the main conduit for the spices coming from the Far East, he allowed the spice trade to fall entirely into Muslim karimi hands by the twelfth century at the expense of the Christian and Jewish merchants, who had formerly made fortunes from that trade. While the Italian city states, descriptively lumped together by the Muslims as Franks, dominated the sea routes of the Mediterranean, the karimi dominated the spice trade and made enormous fortunes in the process.

The rulers of Europe were beating a drum for holy war, and on several occasions the Crusaders provoked Saladin until he finally swore to rid himself of them. In the battle of Hittin in 1187 he dealt a crushing blow. This was followed by a rapid conquest of Palestine until nothing remained of the Crusader strongholds save the port of Tyre and Castle Beaufort in Lebanon. Tyre became the rallying ground for the European monarchs, notably Richard the Lionheart, for the Third Crusade had begun. At the end of five years the Muslims had again driven out the Crusaders, save for a thin strip from Tyre to Jaffa on the coast.

Saladin had achieved his life's work; he had liberated the Holy Land and the city of Jerusalem. The long years of fighting had taken their due; Saladin, never a robust man, succumbed to a fever and died in 1193. He has been described by western authors as 'magnanimous, chivalrous, ascetic, pure in heart and life'. He was the epitome of Muslim chivalry and European knights learned much about chivalry from their gallant enemy. The Crusades in general proved a medium for carrying back to Europe knowledge about medical and scientific practices, for the doctors and scientists of the Middle East were then far in advance of their European counterparts. Thus knowledge of field hospitals, the art of cautery and medicines to cure a variety of fevers, diseases and illnesses were all transmitted to the West.

Saladin's descendants were to rule over Egypt until 1250. After his death a period of infighting among Saladin's sons threatened to destroy the kingdom; finally Safa al-Din, or Safadin, his brother, stepped in, seized power from his incompetent nephews and ruled ably. An exceptionally low Nile in 1201–2 had once again caused famine and distress in the land, and once more historians give accounts of cannibalism, and describe the dread plague which followed famine in an inexorable cycle. Worse was to come when severe earthquakes added to the general misery. Things were so bad with such a high rate of mortality that a single property was said to have passed through the hands of forty heirs within the space of a month.

The Ayyubis were good rulers; they improved the irrigation system, extended canals, dykes and dams, ensured public security so that travellers and commerce were not interfered with, and founded a number of scholarly institutions which were to make Egypt a great intellectual centre.

Another power was rising in the east, that of the Mongol horde under Genghis Khan, and once more the Crusaders recovered power in Palestine, only to be routed again. The penultimate Ayyubi ruler, a man named al-Salih Ayyub, added a new regiment to his army, a regiment of slaves of Turkic origins. He was said to be of a somewhat paranoid nature and distrustful of his regiments; so, thinking to balance their influence by a new force, he bought himself enough slaves to make up a regiment. These slaves, known as *mamluks*, an Arabic word meaning 'owned', were both to save his kingdom and destroy his dynasty at one and the same time.

Al-Salih Ayyub received word that a new Crusade was sailing towards Egypt under the leadership of Louis IX, later to become sanctified. While preparations for the invasion in 1249 were under way, al-Salih died in his tent. His wife, a remarkable woman of Armenian descent, named Shajar al-Durr (Tree of Pearls), connived with the general of the mamluk regiment to keep the news of the ruler's death a secret until the battle was over and his son and heir had returned from abroad to claim his throne. For a month the secret of the ruler's death was kept to prevent the army from becoming demoralized in the midst of an invasion.

The Crusaders landed in Damietta and made the mistake of waiting there until the Nile waters flooded the land and the delta turned into a vast swamp. Then they made their way to the town of Mansura where the mamluk forces were lying in wait for them. On the way the Crusaders suffered from insect bites, fever and intestinal ailments which weakened them, as well as from trying to make their way through swampy land that was alien to them. The Nile at Mansura is very wide, but someone, perhaps a spy, induced Louis's brother, the Comte d'Artois, to follow him to a shallow ford across the river. On Shrove Tuesday, the Comte d'Artois, in too much of a hurry to wait for the rest of the army to catch up with him and his cavalry, forded the river and entered the town of Mansura. There, the mamluk forces, ten thousand strong, under the leadership of a giant of a man named al-Zahir Baibars al-Bunduqdari, or Baibars the Crossbowman, charged the cavalry and cut them to pieces. The flower of Christendom was destroyed and those who were not killed were captured for ransom.

The mamluks had saved Egypt for the last Ayyubi, Turanshah, al-Salih's son, but on his return Turanshah showed little gratitude. He insulted his mamluk generals and humiliated his valiant stepmother who had laboured to set him on the throne. He was soon assassinated by Baibars with the connivance of the mamluks. Shajar al-Durr was chosen by the army to rule over Egypt until her infant son was old enough to rule in his own right, but when the Abbassi ruler wrote the Egyptians an insulting and threatening letter which said, 'If you have no man to rule over Egypt mayhap we can send you one', Shajar al-Durr married Aybak, a mamluk general, as her co-ruler. Her brief reign is unique in the annals of Muslim history, for a woman ruled in her own right and had her name struck on coins – another prerogative of kingship. Shajar al-Durr soon fell out with her husband, for she refused to hand over the treasury to him, and when she poisoned him the mamluks had her killed, thus ending the Ayyubi dynasty and beginning that of the mamluks.

From the age of the mamluks onwards Egypt is again domi- nated by rulers who are alien in ethnicity and in language, for they were Turkic-speaking. Although Egyptians had grown accustomed to military organizations which were entirely Turkic-speaking even when they were manned by non-Turks, which was the norm all along from Abbassi times except for a hiatus under the Fatimis, they now had to face a ruling elite which was also Turkic-speaking in origin. Identification between rulers and ruled was therefore a thing of the past, for where Egyptians could identify with Saladin, a Kurd, it was more difficult to identify with Kipchaks and other foreigners who looked different and brought in different customs and laws. For the mamluks did bring with them the law of the *yasa*, their tribal system, when they took over government in Egypt. The population nevertheless accepted the rule of the mamluks, but did not identify with it, and in most cases they suffered it and survived until better days came round.

2 The age of the mamluks, 1250–1516

A great danger faced the mamluks, that of the advance of the Mongol horde under Hulagu, grandson of Genghis Khan, the man who had razed the fabled city of Baghdad in February 1258 and ended the reign of the Abbassi dynasty over the eastern Muslim world. From then on the focus of Islamic government was to lie with the western Muslim states. Hulagu's forces, unchallenged by any army, moved westward to occupy Syria. The only army capable of standing up to the Mongols were the mamluks of Egypt, who under the leadership of Baibars defeated the Mongols in the battle of Ain Jalut (the Eye of Goliath). Baibars hoped to be rewarded by the governorship of the province of Syria for his victory, but when he was baulked in his ambitions he conspired with other mamluk *amirs* (generals), and they assassinated the mamluk general who had been placed on the throne and replaced him with Baibars in 1260. Baibars, and all the mamluks who followed him on the throne, took on the title of sultan, an Arabic word meaning 'power', and a title which had been used by the Ayyubis. Even after the Abbassi caliphate had been destroyed the mamluks did not use the term 'caliph', which fell into disuse because it was identified with a losing dynasty preferring to continue using the term 'sultan'.

Throughout their period of domination the mamluks were deeply feared and respected by their neighbours because of their martial valour. The mamluk period of government is generally divided into two parts. The first mamluks, who ruled from 1250 to 1382, were named Bahri (river) mamluks, for their barracks lay on the island of Roda, in the River Nile. They were mostly of Turkic origin, as were the Mongols. In fact most of the soldiers of the Middle East from around the tenth century were of Turkic origin, and the language

of the military in consequence was Turkic. The military were generally mercenaries, or mamluks, in the service of some prince or lord,
while the common people sometimes served as auxiliaries but never
served as mercenaries. They were not conscripted into armies until
the nineteenth century. The military profession was therefore one
reserved to a specific group of people: Turk, Kurd, or various other
minorities within the Muslim world who were not native speakers of
Arabic. The second period of mamluk rule was called the rule of the
Burgi (citadel) mamluks because they were quartered in the citadel.
These last were of Turco-Circassian and Greek origin. Mamluks were
bought as boy slaves from the Russian Urals, the Central Asian
steppes or the Caucasus mountains and trained in the households of
older mamluks. Their training included conversion to Islam, and they
were taught Arabic as well, but it mostly concentrated on martial arts
and horsemanship. Once the boys reached the age of puberty they
were manumitted and allowed to grow their beards. Because the
young mamluks were cut off, at an early age, from their families and
people, the focus of their loyalty and affection became the mamluk
household and its members. Affection for the head of the household
as *pater familias*, and for their companions at arms within the household, their siblings in a sense, replaced normal family bonds. On
reaching maturity the mamluks within a household were granted
lands and allowed to set up households of their own; in turn they
bought slaves and perpetuated the system. Alliances were effected
between members of the same household, who joined forces against
mamluks of rival households, so that factionalism became inevitable,
and grew as a result of the system. As the number of households
increased, more opportunities of an economic nature had to be created
to allow a distribution of wealth among the members of the institution. Periodically the numbers of the mamluks were decimated by
plagues or by internecine warfare, so their numbers remained within
the bounds of reason and did not overwhelm the local population.

The early age of the mamluks was characterized by a centralized form of government with one mamluk sultan reigning over the

country and imposing his authority over the rest of the mamluks, who were his retainers in the broad sense. The second period of mamluk government involved a decentralized system where the sultan was not the wielder of authority but was rather a *primus inter pares*, although there were exceptions to that rule and the second period does exhibit sultans who controlled the mamluks strictly and efficiently. But by and large it was a less efficient period of government than the earlier one. The two periods of government gave birth not only to a system of government, but to an institution – the slave oligarchy – that lasted for centuries. The mamluk era gave rise to an age of great aesthetic beauty in its art and architecture and encouraged a flowering of learning by creating schools *(madrasas)* and Sufi monasteries.

The anomaly of an alien elite recruited anew every generation was accepted by the local population because the mamluks showed they were able to defend Egypt against foreign invasions, and because they were armed and ruled over a population that was mostly peasant and unarmed.

Al-Zahir Baibars was the real founder of the Bahri dynasty and the mamluk empire, for all his predecessors had merely been amirs who had ruled for brief periods of time. A Kipchak from the Urals, Baibars was a tall, blue-eyed giant, with a cataract in one eye. He was phenomenally strong and was said to be able to swim across the Nile, which has a strong current, dragging behind him an inflated mattress on which were seated a large number of his mamluks. He was also thoroughly efficient, so the organization he established lasted, as the backbone of mamluk government, for three centuries. He organized the army and the navy, allotted parcels of land *(iqta)* to generals in tenure, and carried out massive public works which benefited the entire population. After the conquest of Syria, his empire stretched from the Taurus mountains to Egypt, and was kept safe and secure by a system of forts and garrisons. The postal system he set up was so efficient it took only a week for a letter to go from Cairo to Damascus. Baibars was also a charitable man who built and endowed schools and mosques. He was an ally of the Byzantine emperor and of the Golden Horde, an alliance which repelled further advances by the Il-Khans, or the Mongols of the east.

All the alliances and treaties Baibars negotiated with neighbouring countries revealed him as a prudent and careful leader, who ruled wisely and well. But there was another side to his nature, one that was adventurous and daring. His exploits so captured the imagination of the Egyptian population that they turned him into a folk hero, writing a romance that recounts his exploits and bears his name. This romance, or the epic tale of Baibars, used to be sung, to the accompaniment of a one-stringed fiddle made out of a coconut shell and a horsetail hair, known as a *rababa,* in all the coffee shops of the country. It was embellished by countless generations of raconteurs until the middle of the twentieth century, when the transistor radio, followed by television, displaced such folk entertainment. His romance however was serialized over the radio, but then displaced by more modern entertainment. The epic tales of Baibars tell how once, before a battle with the Il-Khans, he disguised himself and ventured into a Mongol stronghold to spy out the lie of the land. Once inside the city, he left a ring as a pledge at a pastry-shop where he had dined and the following day wrote to the Il-Khan requesting that he send back his ring, pointing out to the bemused ruler that his fortifications left much to be desired and enumerating the various points of weakness which would allow him, Baibars, to capture the city without the slightest difficulty. The city naturally surrendered without further ado. Baibars had a boon companion who was given to drinking freely, whereas Baibars strictly followed Muslim rules against alcohol. That companion supplied the humorous note that flows alongside the tales of derring-do of the epic.

Baibars died of poison, said to have been prepared by him for an enemy for, while Baibars ruled wisely and well, he also distrusted his followers and knew them to be perfidious and untrustworthy, as he himself had been when he plotted and schemed in the past. On his death his throne was supposed to go to his son, who had none of the father's qualities and was rapidly displaced by one of his father's generals, a man named Qalawun.

Qalawun founded a ruling house that lasted on the throne for a century, and mamluk rule was said to have then reached its apogee with a golden age marked by prosperity and peace. Qalawun's first threat came from the Mongols, who in 1281 attacked his forces in Syria. A battle nearly destroyed the mamluk army when their left flank was defeated by the Mongol right flank, but the mamluk right flank had defeated the Mongol left flank and the tide of battle turned in the mamluks' favour. That victory ushered in a period of armed truce that lasted for seventeen years.

Following Baibars's policies, Qalawun kept an efficient army of strictly disciplined mamluks numbering twelve thousand men. The heads of regiments were referred to as amirs or beys. Though stern and strict, Qalawun was also benevolent towards his subjects. He built the first hospital in Egypt in a complex that included his tomb mosque, a school and a library; both the tomb mosque and the hospital are still in use today. They represent a beautiful example of mamluk architecture, which was highly ornate, colourful and symmetrical in line. It used elaborate calligraphic inscriptions along with stucco decorations to embellish walls and ceilings, had coloured glass windows framed in stucco, and mosaics of multi-coloured stones to decorate walls and floors. The ceilings were enriched with stucco and wood decorations, while a device known as a pendentive allowed for the transition of four walls into a dome, which came to top most mamluk buildings. The hospital had wards for the known diseases of the day, some of which were diagnosed as contagious and isolated. Laboratories, kitchens, a dispensary and baths completed the hospital complex, which also had a regular medical staff. Musicians played in some wards to soothe the ailing, while a library housing a superb collection of medical and pharmaceutical texts assisted the physicians in their endeavours. Rich and poor alike were treated free of charge.

Qalawun's successors were not as benevolent as he had been. One son came to the throne and was so wicked that his generals murdered him. He was then succeeded by a young brother, al-Nasir, who came to the throne on three separate occasions. He was made sultan at the age of nine but deposed after a year. Five years later in 1298 he was brought back to power, but was dominated by the amirs, so that after ten years of abuse at the hands of his commanders he decided to abdicate. Eleven months later he returned to power a third and final time and ruled for a further thirty years. During the interim periods of al-Nasir's reign mamluk amirs succeeded each other on the throne. None lasted for very long for they were soon overthrown by their colleagues. In 1294 a terrible plague swept the country and was associated with the ruler then on the throne. Some Egyptians saw it as an act of divine retribution, for while the country suffered famine the mamluk amir, who was of Mongol origin, had allowed a whole Mongol tribe to immigrate into Egypt and share the scarce supplies of the country when they were not even Muslims. Eventually his amirs conspired against him out of fear of his partiality for the Mongols. The mamluk amirs fought each other, tortured and imprisoned their opponents and carried out atrocities against one another. One amir, named Lajin, was the only one who repealed unjust taxes and so gained the affection of the native population. He was kind to al-Nasir and assured him that he held the throne only until Nasir was old enough to assume government himself. But soon Lajin was murdered by his amirs, and other amirs rose to power. Some disgruntled amirs had fled to the Mongol forces and revealed to them the plight of Egypt, so the Mongols invaded Syria in 1299 seeking to regain territories they had lost to Baibars. After fighting for over three years the Mongols were finally defeated for the fourth time by the mamluks, who devastated the Mongol army so that its chief was said to have died of a broken heart.

During Nasir's early two periods his generals had grown rich and powerful at the expense of the population, and while they tortured and killed each other with impunity they also expended great sums of money in building beautiful mosques and mausoleums, which revealed the magnificence of that period's architecture.

Plagues, famines and an earthquake that almost entirely destroyed the capital marred the years of plenty, but allowed the mamluks to rebuild the damaged buildings and indulge their taste for architecture. Erecting certain buildings is regarded as a benevolent act by Muslims, so that building mosques, schools and drinking fountains was a means of storing up merit. Such buildings were also a form of self-aggrandizement, for people talked about them and the generosity of the man who had caused them to be erected. Whatever the reason, the buildings that had been destroyed by the earthquake were restored and new buildings rapidly appeared, supplying work for the builders and craftsmen of the day.

Nasir's third and last reign from 1310 to 1341 was one of the most brilliant periods of mamluk government, and one of the most felicitous for the common people. Most of the oppressive taxes which had been imposed on the people by his predecessors were repealed. While this occasioned a loss of income to the state, it was made up for by taxing the amirs, who had become excessively wealthy through their previous rapacity. The sultan compelled his amirs to sell their grain in public sales and forbade them to corner the grain market, which they had frequently done in times of famine. Millers and bakers were flogged for overcharging the public, and in times of famine grain was imported from Syria and sold to the public at a fixed price so that no one profited from common misery. Nasir was reported to have punished his own son-in-law when he caught him profiteering and to have struck him for so doing.

The age was one of plenty and well-being, rich in men of learning and of knowledge, such as the historian Abu al-Fida, who was a descendant of Saladin. The sultan and his amirs were prodigal in their wealth and their patronage of the arts, which benefited the artisan population as well as the merchants. Some of the finest museum pieces today date from that period. It is said that Nasir spent 8,000 *dirhams* (silver coins) a day on his buildings. According to historians, his age was the apex of culture and civilization. Nonetheless one can see in the age the seeds of the debacle that was to follow. At times bedouin tribes revolted and took over sections of Upper Egypt, the granary of the land. Mamluk amirs fought each other for a greater share of the spoils, for leadership and power, and in order to continue to do so they extorted large sums of money from the population to enable them to buy arms and slaves to man their households. So long as the land supplied them with the necessary income, their extortions remained within the bounds of reason. Soon they would go beyond those bounds.

The fourteenth century brought the Black Death, which destroyed the old trading system, though that system had begun to show signs of decline long before the plague appeared. The plague appeared in 1347 to 1349 and was said to be so virulent that it carried off one-third of the Egyptian population. Between 1347 and 1513 there were eighteen outbreaks of plague. The consequences were manifold. The population growth of the previous centuries stopped and even declined. Agriculture and the acreage of tilled land shrank, for lack of manpower, to one-fifth of its area prior to the fourteenth century. The land tax dropped to one-tenth of the earlier figure between 1298 and 1517. As a result less food was produced to feed a shrinking population and, more seriously, the mamluk rulers, whose finances depended on agricultural output, had to find other means to complement their waning resources. At the time of the Ayyubis agricultural land had been divided into iqtas given to the military in tenure to defray their salaries and expenses. The mamluks had continued the iqta system so the land tax came to form their only source of income. The search for alternative sources was to have negative repercussions on the country.

Industry and commerce also waned for lack of manpower. The two leading industries in Cairo, sugar making and paper making, diminished, while textile workers, who were said to have numbered 14,000 in 1394, shrank to 800 in 1434, or so the historians of the day inform us. Even if the first figure were exaggerated, the second figure is pretty telling as to the industrial condition of the country. At first the mamluks resorted to taxing the urban communities

THE AGE OF THE MAMLUKS 39

more rapaciously than hitherto, which led to political turmoil and unrest among the mamluks themselves and between them and the population in general. Finally the mamluks monopolized the trade in spices and sugar to pay for their military expenditure and their luxury imports and, by thus establishing a state monopoly of spices and fixing the price of spices sold, they ruined the economic prosperity of the country, albeit for a limited period.

Egypt, which had been inflation-free until the fifteenth century, began to show inflation and a breakdown in the monetary system. Specie, always in short supply, reached critical levels. Europe, which had been drained of its bullion towards the Muslim world to pay for its spices, now saw the flow reversed, with bullion drained from Egypt to pay for furs from the Baltic region, mamluks from the Caucasus to replace those who had been killed by the plague, and weapons. The great profits that had formerly been accumulated through the spice trade evaporated through the purchase of luxury items.

Such was the reputation of al-Nasir and the house of Qalawun that, for forty-one years after his death, twelve of his descendants were placed on the throne as puppet rulers to be manipulated by mamluk amirs who fought each other for supremacy. Finally one amir, stronger than the rest, seized power and brought in the second mamluk period of rule, that of the Burgi mamluks.

The Burgi mamluks ruled from 1382 to 1517. They differed from the Bahri mamluks by virtue of their Circassian and Greek descent, and the fact that they did not follow a hereditary principle in succession. The mamluks elected one of their peers and the new sultan lasted on the throne so long as his talents and skill in manoeuvring his companions held out. His authority depended on alliances with other mamluk households. These alliances were fluid and frequently changed, but they were necessary for the retention of power. Twenty-three sultans came to power, of whom six ruled for a total of 103 years. Only nine sultans were worth remembering; the rest rose and fell very rapidly, and deserved no more than a line, or a footnote, in a chronicle of events.

Though all the sultans had to fight their way to the throne, many among them were also learned men with a highly developed aesthetic sense. We can tell that from the many lovely monuments they left behind, and from the buildings and the fine objets d'art that date from that period.

The rise and fall of Burgi sultans mirrored the internal turmoil that beset the country. The country was frequently beset by revolts, and racked by plague that was followed inexorably by famine. Maqrizi, the most notable historian of the period, claimed that all evil that occurred was due to the corruption and incompetence of the rulers. He accused their government of a lack of continuity which led to political unrest and to turmoil, resulting from the struggles among the amirs as they jockeyed for power every time one of the sultans died, or even when the amirs tired of one sultan and sought to displace him in favour of another who promised them greater spoils. One amir was deposed because he suggested negotiations among warring factions, but the other mamluks thought he was mad to suggest that and deposed him.Finally bedouin encroachments devastated the settled land and caused the fallahin to flee the land, or to become brigands. Brigandage became a threat to the trade routes and diminished commerce.

Such events may have been the consequences rather than the causes of distress in the country. The bedouin may have occupied land already left vacant by the fallahin who had died of plague. Fallahin and bedouin may have taken to brigandage when the tax levels became too high. The rulers, or some among them, were indeed corrupt and incompetent but economic distress can only partially be blamed on them. The Black Death played a great role in bringing about economic hardship. International trade, commerce and population reached a nadir under the mamluks. Frequent civil wars, factional fighting, conspiracy and rebellion did the rest. The population, when squeezed too roughly, countered by rebellion, especially when it saw the lack of unity among the mamluks.

A further Mongol menace was to strike fear into the hearts of the Egyptians for the fifth time. This advance was led by Timurlenk, known in the West as Tamburlaine. Regarded by some as a descendant of the great khans, he was accused by others of being merely a vulgar sheep robber who was wounded during one of his forays, hence his name of Timur the Lame. At first the Egyptian mamluks allied themselves with various princes in the region and with the Ottomans, but when the Ottomans were defeated by Timur things looked bleak for Egypt. Timur despoiled and sacked Damascus, devastated northern Syria, where he was rumoured to have left pyramids of skulls behind him, and put the fear of God into the mamluks. The mamluks sued for terms, so Timur never entered nor even controlled Egypt. One of the men involved in the negotiations with Timur was an eminent scholar, a refugee from Andalusia and the Spanish Inquisition, the father of Arab sociology, ibn Khaldun.

Further wars with amirs in Syria and Anatolia put a heavy burden on the population in terms of taxation and forced loans (avanias). As the mamluks' need for funds grew, along with their campaigns, their rivalries grew in proportion. Some rulers were unable to control their followers, who sacked and looted at will and demanded bribes to support their overlord. These extra funds came from overburdening trade and commerce with taxes, until the final desperate gesture of imposing a monopoly on trade in spices.

The previous dynasts in Egypt had usually added new territory to the country, or regained some lost territory. The mamluks, whose sole talent was warfare, added the island of Cyprus to Egypt under the rule of the Bahri mamluks. The mamluk sultan Barsbay, who ruled from 1422 to 1438, devoted his attention to the Indian trade and managed to squeeze more profits from it than any of his predecessors. However, he taxed the spices at so exorbitant a rate that the Venetians refused to buy from him and sought to repatriate their merchants from Alexandria. Barsbay was then forced to reverse his terms and become more reasonable. Inflation grew during his period not only because of poor economic conditions, but also because he debased the coinage. Another sultan accepted bribes from amirs which allowed them to torture other amirs. Finally they decided to go ahead with torturing each other without having to pay the sultan a fee for the privilege.

Sultan Qaitbay enjoyed the longest reign of any mamluk sultan since al-Nasir, ruling for twenty-nine years from 1468 to 1496. He managed to subdue the other mamluk amirs, frequently flogging some of them with his own powerful hands. He embarked on a series of campaigns which necessitated extracting funds from the amirs as well as from the population at large, so land was taxed at the rate of three-tenths of its produce. He was also a prolific builder of roads, bridges, mosques, schools and forts not only in Egypt but in the other territories of his empire, Syria, Mecca and Jerusalem. Any crumbling monument was restored by him, making the list of his restorations and constructions a long one. Someone had to pay the price for restoring these exquisite buildings, and this called for further acts of oppression by the ruler. However, the building programme necessitated hiring an army of workers, artisans, builders and masons, so perhaps these public works were also a means of supplying work for some of the population. During that period a number of Sufi monasteries were built, and Sufi adherents grew. It may well be that these monasteries were also a means of gathering potential malcontents and redirecting their energies towards a life of contemplation rather than towards a life of struggle against the authorities. The mamluks generously endowed monasteries, but whether they did so for the reason given or hoped to buy salvation in the afterlife is questionable.

The reign of Qaitbay saw the restoration of economic prosperity. Although the spice trade, or East–West trade, had decreased along with trade in luxury goods, trade in everyday commodities such as linen, rice, cereals, leather and sugar increased.

An exceptionally deadly plague swept over Egypt in 1492 and was said to have carried off twelve thousand a day in Cairo. This plague killed off many mamluks, who were more susceptible to the disease than were native-born Egyptians. It may be that they had not had time to develop immunity, since they were newly imported into the country. Perhaps because the mamluks wore more clothes, where plague-infested fleas could reside, or lived in richer furnishings which could house a greater number of vectors, or perhaps because historians lived in cities and could count more mamluks than fallahin – whatever the reason, mamluks died in large quantities. The plague was followed by a cattle disease which killed off the main animals used for ploughing. A serious outbreak of civil strife, pitting two groups of mamluks against each other, crowned the calamities. Qaitbay, said to be worn out by these events, died and a period of strife and chaos followed, until one amir, Qansuh al-Ghuri, finally seized power in 1501 and instituted a more repressive regime than ever before. Qansuh, whose name had become a byword in popular parlance for anyone displaying overweening arrogance and conceit, restored order, but levied ten months' taxes and confiscated lands which were held in trust for charity. He raised customs duties, debased the coinage further but replenished the treasury.

By the end of the fifteenth century the Ottomans had once again become a mighty force, expanding in Europe, but also in Asia, so their territories bordered those of the mamluks to the north. By then the mamluks were losing power militarily and were soon to be overwhelmed by the rising power of the Ottomans. The Ottoman sultan had captured the northern territories of Syria and the Euphrates. The ruler of Persia, Shah Ismail, the Safavi monarch, had made overtures to the mamluk sultan, inviting him to join with the Persian forces and unite to defeat the Ottoman army. Had al-Ghuri indeed consented to such a union, the combined armies might perhaps have defeated the forces of Sultan Selim the Grim, but al-Ghuri, who was growing old and tired of war, turned down the offer, believing the Ottomans would leave him alone if he offered them no provocation. The Ottomans defeated the Safavis in battle at Chaldiran and then turned their attention to the mamluk-held dominions.

Ghuri was over seventy years old and long past his fighting days. He rode out to battle in May 1516 and made a triumphal entrance into Damascus. Selim assured him that he had no intention of attacking the Egyptian forces, but the two forces met on the battlefield in the plain of Marj Dabiq north of Aleppo on 24 August 1516 and the mamluk forces suffered a resounding defeat.

The Ottomans had a larger battle-seasoned army, which had seen a number of campaigns; the mamluk army of the day had seen only petty, local squabbles. In addition the Ottomans were experienced in the use of artillery and firearms. The mamluks were a cavalry regiment that prided itself on its equestrian talents. A cavalry officer could only use the firearms of the day in a limited fashion, while artillery on horseback was out of the question. The mamluks did have an artillery unit but they used it only in static warfare, as in besieging or defending a city. The notion of bringing men to the battlefield in bullock carts to man artillery pieces was anathema to the mamluks. Furthermore firearms shot from a galloping horse were worse than useless, whereas hand-to-hand combat was the essence of cavalry units. The Ottomans on the other hand were experienced in the use of artillery and gunpowder; their main source of strength lay in their infantry, armed with firearms, the *spahis* or cavalry having outlasted their utility on the battlefield. To make sure that superior fighting power would not be overcome by any untoward elements, the Ottomans ensured their victory by bribing Khair Bey, al-Ghuri's second-in-command.

Described as the most brilliant cavalry of the age, the mamluks entered battle expecting to face the enemy in a normal hand-to-hand combat at which they excelled, and for which they had been trained. Instead they were met by a deadly hail of gunpowder that decimated their ranks before they even got within hailing distance of the enemy. Mamluks who were captured alive raged at the Ottomans, asking them to give them a fighting chance, to fight like men in hand-to-hand combat instead of aiming these fire-spewing instruments at them. The Ottomans, who were not fighting a war for fun, but for profit, contemptuously laughed at the mamluks who believed there was a code of honour in fighting a war which had to be respected or the soldier disgraced.

The Ottomans won the day through superior technology, but also through a rumour that al-Ghuri had been killed. Without a leader, faced with cannon and guns and led by a second-in-command who counselled surrender, many of the mamluks ran from the battlefield to carry the tale of defeat back to their countrymen. Al-Ghuri had indeed been killed on the battlefield, but the rumour had been spread before his death by Khair Bey and may indeed have caused his death when his forces ran from battle.

Back in Egypt the mamluks elected a new leader. They chose one of al-Ghuri's former slaves, a man named Tuman Bey. Selim sent Tuman a letter suggesting he rule as viceroy under Ottoman suzerainty, and Tuman was tempted to accept the offer, since it merely involved reciting the name of the Ottoman sultan during the Friday prayers, minting coins with the sultan's name, and paying some form of tribute, to be arranged later between the two parties. The rest of the mamluks refused these terms in high dudgeon and, adding insult to imprudence, they killed Selim's messenger. The outcome was a foregone conclusion and on 23 January 1517 the Ottomans defeated the mamluks and entered the city of Cairo. Sultan Selim learned all the information he needed to know about the government of Egypt from Tuman Bey and then had him hanged from one of the southern gates of Cairo, Bab Zuwaila. The new viceroy of Egypt was the same Khair Bey who had been bribed by the Ottomans, and who was now rewarded for his perfidy by being given high office. The Egyptians, who like making puns, immediately named the new viceroy Khain Bey, a pun on the man's name, for while Khair means 'good' Khain means 'traitor'.

The former mamluk empire was now divided into three sections. The northern regions (the Syrian provinces closest to the Ottoman boundaries) became the governorate of Aleppo. The southern areas centred round Damascus formed the second province, while Egypt, with Cairo as its capital, became the third province or governorate. Khair was appointed governor for life as a vassal of the sultan rather than as a provincial governor on yearly tenure, the usual Ottoman practice. The revenues of Egypt were granted to him as a tax-farm, although the country had to pay a tribute as well. Although

Khair was tenured for life, like other Ottoman governors his tenure had to be officially renewed every year.

Four regiments of the Ottoman army, known as *ocaks*, were left behind to control Egypt. Foremost among the ocaks were the Janissaries, the crack infantry regiment, which was credited with having won most of the victories for the Ottoman empire. At some later stage three further ocaks were added to those already stationed in Egypt, formed primarily of former mamluks.

The rule of the mamluks had been a mixed blessing for the Egyptians. While the early period of Bahri mamluks had largely been a prosperous and felicitous period for the people, the later period had been frequently oppressive and chaotic, although periods of prosperity did follow periods of disaster and epidemics. The native Egyptians, in spite of being viewed as chattel by the later mamluks, nonetheless retained an identity as pertaining to a land, Egypt, which was an independent kingdom, and at times was the centre of a mamluk empire with all that that implies in terms of prosperity, prestige, and patronage of artisans and of intellectuals. Thus it had been a centre for intellectual and artistic developments and a source of inspiration to intellectuals and artists in other Muslim countries, many of whom flocked to Egypt to learn in the madrasas that were so generously endowed by the mamluks, and in the Sufi monasteries, which also served as centres of learning. Even though they endowed centres of learning and religious teaching, historians tell us that the mamluks, who were nominally Muslims, frequently behaved like pagans in their rapacity and abuse of Muslims.

The mamluk form of government allowed a son to succeed his father as the head of the state, but in only one case, that of al-Nasir, do we have a son succeeding his father and lasting on the throne for any length of time, so that the system of succession depended more on military strength than upon a legal institution. Continuity of government was thus rarely maintained, and the changes made by different and successive rulers made for a precarious and disjointed form of government. However, this was to be the last independent government Egypt was to have for a long time, for legally Egypt was to become an Ottoman province and remain vassal to the Ottomans until 1914.

The mamluks had outlived their usefulness and effectiveness as a fighting force and were displaced by an army that had acquired the latest technology of the day and which in consequence had easily defeated them. The mamluks however were never displaced completely by the Ottomans, who soon grew to rely upon them in administering Egypt, and they were to return to power and once again rule over Egypt.

Once more Egypt was relegated to the status of a mere province within a larger empire, an empire that was similar in religion but different in language and ethnicity. The alienation between rulers and ruled was to continue. Because the Ottomans had not subdivided Egypt into separate provinces but had maintained it as one province, it continued as an entity that was separated from the other provinces of the Ottoman empire, even though subject to that empire and sharing religious and linguistic affinity with the other Arab provinces. Soon enough that distance from the empire was to cause some mamluks to turn their thoughts to autonomy.

3   The Ottoman age, 1516–1805

Khair Bey ruled as the Ottoman viceroy *(wali)* until his death in 1522. The viceroy, or governor of the province, was frequently given the rank of *pasha* – although Khair Bey was not – from then on all governors are referred to as pashas, while the mamluks are collectively referred to as the beys or amirs. Within two years of Khair's death a revolt broke out and the new Ottoman sultan, Sulaiman the Lawgiver, as he was known to his own people, or the Magnificent, as he was known to the Western world, sent his grand vizier to suppress the revolt and to establish a form of administration that was spelled out in an edict, the *qanunname*. With minor modifications, that system of government remained in practice in Egypt until the eighteenth century.

According to the edict Egypt was divided into fourteen provinces covering the delta and Upper Egypt, each province administered by a government agent responsible to the wali. Upper Egypt, ranging from the town of Asiut to the southern borders, was administered by Arab tribal *sheikhs* acting as government agents. These tribal rulers continued to enjoy authority over the region until 1576, when a bey was finally appointed governor over the region. The concentration of bedouin tribes in Upper Egypt made tribal authority a viable (and cheaper) alternative to stationing government forces in the area.

The viceroy headed the administration of the entire province of Egypt and was appointed by the sultan from the imperial capital. He was required to hold a council *(diwan)* four times a week, patterned on the sultan's own diwan. That diwan in Egypt was one of the unusual features of the administration and was supposed to incorporate the regimental heads, local leaders – both religious and commercial – and the chief judge *(qadi)*, also nominated from Istanbul, as representatives of all the interests in the province. The second unusual feature was that the land was not parcelled out as areas given over to military regiments in return for military service, but was divided into plots and farmed out for taxes, a method known as *iltizam*. At a later period the iltizam was put up for auction to the highest bidder and the tax-farmer *(multazim)* paid a fee for the right to collect the taxes. By the eighteenth century tax-farmers had become virtual landowners and could pass the land on to their heirs or buy and sell the right to a tax-farm, so for all intents and purposes land had become private property.

For the next sixty years the country lay quiescent under Ottoman military rule, but economic difficulties were soon to beset the Ottoman empire and to have repercussions on the economic situation in Egypt. These events were the consequences of the price revolution that occurred in the sixteenth century, caused by the flow of cheap silver from the New World. This upset the balance of exchange between gold and silver in the Ottoman empire, debased the Ottoman currency and caused general inflation. Salaries of troops, which had been fixed, one of the great innovations of the Ottomans, were rendered almost worthless through inflation and were certainly insufficient. This led to abuses in both government and administration as the army and the administration sought to compensate for the losses suffered through devaluation and inflation by resorting to other, extra-legal means.

Currency devaluation led the Ottoman regiments in Egypt to rebel against the governor and to demand rises, for they could no longer live on their salaries. The first rebellion took place in 1586 after sixty years of peaceful government. Other rebellions followed, for whatever steps were taken proved insufficient to placate the soldiery. A rebellion in 1609 was so violent it could only be put down after a great deal of fighting. The new walis who were sent out to Egypt every time a rebellion occurred soon found themselves in an anomalous position. Legally the wali had no control over the regiments, who were subject to their regimental commanders and were not under the jurisdiction of the wali. The governor, who might have arrived in the country with new forces, saw these same forces join up with the rebellious regiments and make common cause with them. Soon the governors came to rely on mamluk forces to help them against the regiments. The wali had to resort to balancing factions against one another in order to get things done.

By now the mamluks in Egypt were probably descendants of the old mamluk amirs of the previous dynasty, for the system continued to perpetuate itself. Mamluk beys continued to buy young slaves to replenish their households, except that now the new mamluks came from new areas – they were Bosniaks, Greeks, or even Arabs. Though used in the Ottoman administration, the mamluks had not been given specific functions and so were able to serve in a variety of positions, wherever they were needed. Their knowledge of the land and of its traditions rendered them indispensable; slowly but surely they infiltrated all branches of the administration. The Ottomans had even formed three regiments from among the mamluks to supplement the four Ottoman regiments in the country. Because of the system of households, the mamluks had a greater degree of cohesiveness than perhaps the Ottoman regiments had, for all those belonging to the same household had developed quasi-fraternal bonds towards each other. The mamluk beys were equally devoted to the interests of the members of their households and tried to place them in key positions; eventually a network was developed, encompassing all members of the household.

The revolt in 1609 was led by mamluk beys and by the Ottoman regiments which had been formed out of the remnants of the mamluk regiments. That gave the revolt the air of a separatist movement designed by mamluks to overthrow the authority of the Ottoman regiments, which is why it was described as a second conquest of the country. The Ottomans managed to suppress the movement, but it was to surface again in the eighteenth century.

Even though that rebellion had been suppressed, mamluks continued to hold political authority in the land; it was from among them that high political and military officers were chosen. It may be that the Ottomans could not spare men to send out to Egypt, and so preferred to use local talent. Thus a mamluk became the person who led the yearly pilgrimage caravan to Mecca *(amir al-hajj)*. As a state functionary, amir al-hajj was endowed with sufficient funds to raise an army that was to protect the caravan, the richest and most prestigious one, on its way to the Hijaz. By virtue of that position, a leading mamluk bey was financed by the central government to develop a standing army of his own in order to guard the caravan. A second prestigious position was the leader of the caravan that carried the yearly tribute to Istanbul; that, too, went to a mamluk bey. Lastly the head of the financial administration *(defterdar)* was also appointed from among the mamluks.

The mamluks' authority became so extensive that they took to deposing any unpopular governor and set up interim governors of their own choice until a new candidate was sent out from the imperial capital. That occurrence became so frequent that it was institutionalized. All the beys had to do was send one messenger on donkey back, who rode up to the pasha's residence in the citadel, entered his audience chamber, folded back an edge of the carpet in the room and said, 'Descend, oh pasha.' Whereupon the governor had no option but to pack his baggage and leave the land on pain of death. Since the governor had no armed force at his command, save for a troop of fifty men, he had no alternative and obeyed.

For the next twenty-five years until 1656 one mamluk bey, Ridwan Bey al-Fiqari, was the real ruler of Egypt, while the Ottoman wali, who was appointed on yearly tenure, simply remained a figurehead, who sat out his year's service, made whatever money he could and returned to the capital at the end of the year. On Ridwan's death a rival mamluk faction tried to gain the ascendancy and the Ottoman walis who were sent out to govern rapidly realized their opportunity for acquiring some degree of power by playing one mamluk faction off against the other. In the process the mamluk factions were weakened, and by 1644 mamluk power had waned sufficiently to enable the power of the Ottomans to rise once again, even though mamluks con-tinued to play a role in the administration.

With the decline of the mamluk grandees, we see the rise to power not of the wali but of the Janissary regiment and its leaders. A series of uprisings then pitted the younger officers against their senior officers, and rebellions broke out in 1698, 1706 and in 1707 (lasting until 1711). This last long rebellion was dubbed 'The Great Insur-rection' for obvious reasons and was, to all intents and purposes, a civil war among the elite. The native population was not directly involved in all these troubles.

During the period when the regiments were in the ascendancy, the soldiers, suffering as they did from inflation and from fixed sala-ries, had tried to supplement their dwindling incomes by establishing a symbiotic relationship with the artisans. In the urban areas artisans and merchants were grouped into trade corporations or guilds. The soldiers fraternized with the artisans and in return for protecting them from the government they levied a protection fee. Soon they intermarried with the local population and became artisans them-selves. The soldiers became so Egyptianized that artisans and mer-chants joined the ranks of the Janissaries and the other Ottoman regiments, and by the end of the seventeenth century it became diffi-cult to tell an artisan from a soldier. The mutual advantages of such an alliance were that the regiments prevented the administration from laying too heavy a tax burden on the artisans, and from exploit-ing them through forced loans and *avanias,* while at the same time the soldiers earned a fee from the artisans and acquired a new profes-sion. In due course the regiments became entitled to a 10 per cent fee levied on the inheritance of any artisan or merchant who died, which supplemented regimental salaries quite comfortably. The regiments therefore built an economic base through the exploitation of urban guilds. On the other hand the mamluks were building their economic base through the exploitation of rural tax-farms, which more and more fell under their control, until the eighteenth century when financial need drove them to seek alternative forms of finance.

Need for money was also due to rising inflation. We can trace the rate of inflation by examining the rate of exchange of the local currency, the smallest coin of which was the copper *para*, the equivalent of the Ottoman *asper* (*akce*). From 1681 to 1688 the para remained stable, but from then on there was a rapid devaluation of currency, and by 1791 the para was worth 47 per cent of its value a century earlier. Such monetary distress was closely linked to the crises within the Ottoman empire in the seventeenth and eighteenth centuries, though some of it was due to internal and local conditions, as well as to the international commercial situation.

Through continuous interregimental fighting the regiments soon lost their leaders and became so weakened that the mamluks once again stepped into the power vacuum and reasserted their ascendancy over the regiments and over the country. The system of rule by mamluk grandees, the beys, which was known as the beylicate, was to last until the French occupation of Egypt in 1798.

The internal revolts of the regiments were a consequence of rivalry over income-producing resources. From the outset each Ottoman regiment had been assigned a series of urban tax-farms whose income was supposed to supply the salaries for the members of the regiment. As we have seen, the tax-farms, having proved insufficient, were supplemented by cooperation with the artisans and their guilds. Until 1730 trade and commerce was sufficiently profitable to defray the needs of the ruling elite. Profits mostly came from the coffee trade which enabled merchants to accumulate immense fortunes, akin to the fortunes of the karimi merchant princes of the Middle Ages. Textile production was another source of income. The main trade routes were those going to the Hijaz, where coffee, spices and textiles from India were obtained and shipped to Egypt, whence they were sold to the Ottoman empire and Syria, to Europe, the Sudan and North Africa. Egyptian trade was one of entrepot trade transferring commodities imported from one country and exported to another. Apart from trade with the Hijaz, which was most lucrative, there was trade with the Ottoman empire, which formed the second major trade route. Trade with Europe provided only one-seventh of the total trade of the country. French merchants bought coffee, brought to Egypt from the Hijaz, and bought Egyptian textiles which they distributed throughout Europe.

By 1730 French merchants were beginning to produce coffee in the Antilles in sufficient quantities to displace Mocha coffee from the Hijaz and significantly to affect the flow of wealth derived from the coffee trade. While Antillean coffee was not as savoury as Mocha coffee, it was considerably cheaper and soon took over the European market. Even the Ottomans, who at first had proscribed the sale of Antillean coffee within their dominions, soon began to buy it. Mocha continued to be a sought-after item, but was no longer a massive moneymaker. The same held true for Egyptian textiles, which during the early eighteenth century had formed 60 per cent of Egyptian exports to Europe. Textiles were displaced by French goods, which flooded the market, while France placed an edict against importing foreign cloth which fell below a certain specified width, which could only be obtained by using the new, wider looms that the French had invented.

Strife among the beys was commonplace as they jockeyed for power which led to greater wealth. Each household sought to attract to itself a greater share of wealth from the dwindling fund of commercial and urban taxation. To gain an edge over their rivals, mamluk households began to import weaponry from Europe; and to pay for such an expensive item a more extensive tax system was imposed on the population. This need for weaponry, and for luxury imports as well, came at a time when rural tax-farms were no longer able to provide the beys with all the funds they needed, so they turned to urban areas for supplementary sources of income. They displaced the regiments in their hold over urban taxes and, realizing that an alliance with artisans would be of little use, they allied themselves with the *tujjar* (long-distance merchants), the financial and commercial elite. Together tujjar and mamluks formed an alliance for trade and profit. Hence, while the richer elements in the country were united in joint pursuits, the poorer elements – the artisans and regiments – were to suffer the consequences. The tujjar wanted to be paid for the weapons and luxury items the mamluks imported and, as coffee and textiles had diminished in value, they sought to find new commodities for export which would pay for the imports. These commodities were to be raw materials which Europe began to demand in greater quantities as she embarked on her industrial revolution. Tujjar and mamluks thus conspired to deny local artisans raw materials by raising the price of raw cotton, but maintaining the price of textiles, making it uneconomic for the artisans to go on weaving textiles for the local market. Cotton, rice, and sugar began to be grown in commercial quantities for the export market.

Land, which had been the main source of funding for the beys, was yielding less money than before. Most of the mamluks of the later period were absentee landlords, unlike their earlier predecessors who had lived on the land. The absentee landlords employed the native rural elite, the *ayan*, to act as their agents in the countryside. The ayan diverted to their own use a portion of the money derived from the tax-farms, which diminished the portion reaching the mamluks. It is true the mamluks imposed heavier taxes on the fallahin, but there was a limit beyond which they could not go for fear of losing their peasantry, who would run away from the land and the heavy taxes.

As mamluk need for money grew, they began to sell their ownership of tax-farms to those elements in the country who had ready cash, that is to merchants, men of religion *(ulama)* and to women. The merchants were clearly not the only group in the country to have control over cash in large quantities. They were also keen on diversifying their holdings to minimize any future financial catastrophe. Some of them were also interested in increasing the amount of crops that could be exported and so invested in land as a means of turning simple farming into commercial farming for export. The ulama were another element in the country that had means. Though many of the ulama were poor, the high ulama were rich, for they were overseers of charitable endowments and had control over their funds. They were also remunerated by the regiments in cash or in grain, which they then sold, and were involved in trade and commerce in partnership with the tujjar. Ulama, as well as tujjar, became interested in possessing land. The third group, women, were mostly the wives, daughters or widows of mamluks who had inherited tax-farms from their male relatives. Women, who were wives and daughters of ulama and merchants, were also involved in trade and commerce, and had enough cash to pay for tax-farms.

Such a transfer of tax-farms from the hands of mamluks and regimental commanders to the hands of new groups of tax-farmers leads us to assume that by the first third of the eighteenth century land was slowly becoming a commodity that could be bought, sold and alienated, although this was not officially acknowledged. Furthermore the new elites in the rural milieu and the new landlords – merchants, men of religion and women – fearing that a turn of the wheel might lead to the confiscation of their properties, began to turn land into a sort of endowment in perpetuity *(waqf)*. These mortmain endowments could not be confiscated legally, for in essence they were endowed for a charitable purpose. Such endowments could be for pure charity, as in endowing a mosque, a school or a mausoleum, or they could be a means of alienating land in perpetuity to prevent legal heirs from selling or mortgaging the land. That last kind was a waqf of a private nature, which also had clauses specifying charitable works of some sort. It was through endowments that all the social services of the country were financed, as well as education and learning at all levels. Many of the lands alienated as waqf were illegally converted, for in theory land could be turned into waqf only with the approval of the sultan or the highest legal authorities. Nonetheless one-fifth of the agricultural land of Egypt (roughly half a million *faddans* or acres) had been transformed into waqf. Waqf lands were generally not taxed or were taxed at a very low rate which explained the attraction of the system.

In brief, at a time when the mamluks needed more money to enable them to wage battles against each other as they struggled for ascendancy, they were faced with a decline in agricultural revenue, and a decline in commercial revenue resulting from losses in trading commodities such as coffee. Alternative means of raising money were necessary. These means led to the imposition of greater degrees of taxation on the urban workers, plus periodic levies, avanias and confiscations when the need grew acute. The regiments were no longer in a condition to defend the artisans from exploitation, for they were dominated by the beys, who milked the population for all it was worth.

From the middle of the eighteenth century we notice a new title applied to the leading mamluk bey, *sheikh al-balad* (chief of the country, or in another context it might mean village headman). This was not an Ottoman title, although the Ottomans came to recognize and accept it and to use it in their correspondence with the Egyptian administration when referring to the actual wielder of authority in the country, the head of all the mamluk beys. With the advent of that title we see hints of an attempt at centralization on the part of the mamluks, with one bey dominating the rest for a limited period. Struggles among beys however continued until 1768, when one mamluk finally seized power and established his rule as sheikh al-balad more successfully than any of his predecessors. This was Ali Bey al-Kabir, also known as Bulut Kapan, or Cloud Catcher, a nickname given to him because of his grandiose schemes. Ali Bey was not content to become the supreme ruler of Egypt. He also determined to make the country independent of Ottoman domination and to expand it into an empire by conquering countries that bordered Egypt, the Hijaz and Syria, as so many former governors of Egypt had done in the past.

In order to carry out his schemes for expansion, Ali Bey had to impose his authority over the other mamluk households, and no pocket of opposition was allowed to exist within the country. He did this either by killing his opponents from among the grandees or by exiling them. Being in a great hurry to accomplish his designs, he could not wait until young slaves grew older and were trained in the

arts of warfare, so he bought an army of mercenaries, thereby changing the mamluk system of recruitment by importing grown men who
felt little loyalty to a household or to a country in which they had just
landed. A centralized authority to replace the previous loose system
of alliances among households which characterized the period of
mamluk domination known as the beylicate, a system which shifted
with changing perceptions, had to be established. The new ruler
appointed his own men as governors over the fourteen provinces of
Egypt; thus a budding bureaucracy and administrative hierarchy with
a chain of command leading to one man was in the making. To establish his sole rule Ali Bey had to destroy the Arab tribal sheikhs who
controlled the resources of Upper Egypt, for they could threaten the
security of the capital and starve it through withholding the grain
which fed the cities. Lastly he had to establish control over the tujjar
and control trade and commerce, thereby diverting their resources
and incomes to himself. In the past, customs dues and levies had also
been turned into tax-farms which defrayed the expenses of either the
governor or the regiments. Ali Bey appointed new customs officials
from among recent Syrian emigrés, who showed him new ways of
taxing trade and allowed him a more stringent control of these
resources. The old customs officials had been Jews, who had a close
alliance with the regiments and who were thus distrusted by Ali Bey.
The most important means of controlling trade and commerce was to
occupy those countries that fed into the most lucrative trade routes,
notably the Hijaz and Syria. The occupation of the Hijaz was rapidly
carried out, but the campaign in Syria brought him on a collision
course with the Ottomans, who controlled Syria.

A few centuries earlier the Ottoman army had defeated the
mamluk army through its use of gunpowder, a skill the mamluks had
acquired but had not perfected. Ali Bey laboured to remedy that dis-
advantage and tried to instruct his army in the use of gunpowder technology; he even armed ships with cannon bought from the Russians,
the enemies of the Ottomans. This was to no avail; history repeated
itself, for the Ottomans played the same game as in earlier times and

bribed Ali Bey's second-in-command. Ali Bey was deposed by his own men and had to flee for his life. He sought refuge for a while with an Arab tribe, but his erstwhile companions could not rest until he was found and captured in 1773.

From then onwards Egypt continued to be ruled by mamluks who had a precarious hold on power, for they had no local power base and had to rely on their own militias, who were fickle and demanded constant bribes as the price of their support. Such demands increased the need to exploit the population even further. A series of popular uprisings once every ten or fifteen years in protest at too great a tax burden occurred in both the rural and urban areas. No strong hand replaced Ali Bey, so coalitions and factions eventually led to the government of Egypt by a duumvirate of beys, neither of whom was strong enough to rule in his own right.

A series of low Niles brought hunger and want to the country, followed by epidemics of a virulent nature. Once again chroniclers recounted tales of people eating one another or eating carcasses of animals lying in the streets. The fallahin flocked in from the country-side seeking food in the cities and died in the streets, for there was no food there either. The land was left untenanted, and could produce no crops for the following seasons. Some of the artisans had been ruined by the merchants, who had tried to stop local artisanal work in order to export the raw materials to Europe, which needed the commodities for its expanding industries; these displaced artisans became an unemployed proletariat. The merchants were not doing well either because of rising competition and diminishing resources. The ground was set for a change. By then the population had dropped to about three million, while the amount of land under cultivation had also decreased for lack of manpower.

A change was to come in the shape of the French occupation of Egypt at the hands of Napoleon Bonaparte in 1798. Napoleon, accom-panied by some fifty scientists and savants, as well as by a large and seasoned army that had seen battle in Europe, landed in Egypt with the intention of setting up a French colony, as the French were to do with greater success in Algeria in 1830. At first the mamluks put up some resistance, as did the population, but in the face of cannon and the Old Guard (which seemed to duplicate the events of 1516 when the mamluks had to face the Ottomans), they turned tail and fled, some to Gaza and some to Upper Egypt where they controlled the grain resources. The French never managed to establish control over the whole country, for as they gave chase to the mamluks the latter fled further south into the Sudan and returned as soon as the French army evacuated the region. The French had neither the resources nor the manpower to station garrisons all over the country, and ended by controlling little more than the capital and parts of the delta. Their situation in Egypt was generally precarious. The French fleet had been sunk by Lord Nelson in the Bay of Abuqir, the campaign of Acre was a disaster, and plague devastated the army in Palestine. Over a year after landing in Egypt Napoleon deserted his men and secretly left Egypt to return to France and organize the *coup d'état* that brought him to power.

The French army was left behind to cope as best it could, without a fleet to provide it with supplies, and with little hope of being evacuated. General Kléber, whom Napoleon had left in charge, did the best he could, but he had no desire to remain in Egypt, and neither did his army. Eventually he came to an understanding with the mamluks to supply him with grain from Upper Egypt in return for his recognizing their right to rule there. Kléber had to face a local uprising and was finally assassinated by a Syrian from Aleppo.

Kléber was succeeded by General Jacques Menou, who took Napoleon's plan for making Egypt a province of France quite seriously, unlike Kléber who only thought of returning home. He set about reforming the administration and establishing a chain of command. Menou had converted to Islam and married the daughter of a bathhouse keeper in Rosetta in the mistaken idea that he was marrying into Egyptian aristocracy because his wife's family were descended from the Prophet. He became a figure of fun both to his own men, who wanted nothing more than to leave Egypt and return to France where all the excitement was brewing, and to the Egyptians, who sniggered at the way he treated his wife as though she were a Frenchwoman.

In conjunction with the British, the Ottomans finally roused themselves in 1801 to organize an expedition to oust the French from Egypt. The Anglo-Ottoman forces managed to force the French to evacuate the country and left the Ottomans in nominal control. The mamluks assumed they would be reinstated in their former positions of authority, and the British forces supported that interpretation for they believed they could manipulate the mamluks to their own advantage. On the other hand the Ottomans assumed their presence in Egypt would develop a new form of government and cause the end of the mamluks, who had given the Ottomans a great deal of trouble and no small anxiety over the past decades, and who frequently neglected to send the tribute to the imperial capital, pleading lack of funds. The native population, which under the French occupation had grown to depend on their natural leaders, the ulama, whom Napoleon had gathered into a diwan to help rule the country, found themselves caught in the crossfire between the two warring factions.

The French conquest of Egypt had broken the ties that had bound the mamluks to the local population. The reason the Egyptians put up with the mamluks, other than the fact that they did not have the military means of getting rid of them, was a belief that at least the mamluks would protect them from foreign invasion of any kind. That reason proved to be fictitious, for the mamluks were incapable of any military effectiveness. The Egyptian leaders, the ulama, men of religion who had been entrusted with administrative functions by the French, even though these functions were not of their own choosing, began to see that an alternative to mamluk rule in Egypt was feasible, if only they could find the proper person. That person soon appeared in the shape of a young officer, who had landed in Egypt among the Albanian contingent that formed one of the two wings of the Ottoman army, a man named Muhammad Ali, who was to change the history of Egypt.

Muhammad Ali rapidly rose from the position of a minor officer to become second-in-command of the Albanian mercenaries. When the leader of the Albanians was assassinated by the Ottomans in a power struggle, he became their commander-in-chief. Between 1801 and 1805 Egypt suffered a turbulent period when Ottomans, mamluks and British forces tried to put their candidates in power as governors of Egypt.

The Ottomans appointed governors who were rapacious, incapable and had little authority over their own soldiers. The Ottoman soldiers treated the land as though it were conquered territory, sacking and looting at will. Having suffered through a French occupation and a consequent cessation of trade for the past three years, the Egyptians found things becoming worse for the next three years, when they had been 'liberated' by their suzerain. Whatever commercial activity had existed came to a rapid halt. The exactions of the Ottomans were severe, to the extent that soldiers plundered people's houses; they kidnapped women from the streets and the public baths, and simply took anything they fancied without paying for it. Their excuse was that their salaries had not been paid them by their officers. On the other hand the Ottoman administrators and the mamluk beys were taxing the population by turns, each claiming the taxes were rightfully due to them. The Ottomans tried to set a trap for the mamluks in order to exterminate them, and the latter only escaped through British intervention. In brief, the military were all fighting each other for power; one governor was assassinated and his successor was promptly murdered in his turn. The situation could best be described as chaotic.

Throughout that period, while the population suffered the ravages of a second occupation, the natural leaders of the country, the ulama, were consorting with the only man who seemed to know what he was doing, and who talked in sensible terms. That man was Muhammad Ali, who ingratiated himself with the ulama, especially with the marshal of the notables, a man called Sayyid Umar Makram. At first Muhammad Ali had befriended one faction of mamluks and had risen to prominence and into the public eye through that alliance. Next he approached the ulama, telling them that Egypt could become rich and prosperous if she were properly governed. The ulama and the merchants, who had been impoverished through inactivity and exactions, listened to Muhammad Ali and became convinced that he represented the alternative leadership which they had been looking for. The situation became desperate when an Ottoman governor, unable to control his soldiery, imported a troop of soldiers from Syria. These soldiers, known as the Delhis, or madmen, were notorious for their high astrakhan bonnets and their lack of discipline. Made up of Druze, Nusairis and Matawila, they were worse than anything the Egyptians had seen before. They attacked villages, raped the women and carried them and the children off along with anything else that was movable.

In desperation the ulama conferred with Muhammad Ali and asked him to become governor of Egypt, according to the will of the people, so long as he undertook to govern in accordance with their advice, and abide by their norms, that is, that he would agree to rule in consultation with the ulama. He accepted the offer and the ulama galvanized the local population of Cairo into besieging the Ottoman governor in the citadel and proclaiming Muhammad Ali governor of Egypt. The Ottoman governor resisted, saying that he was named by the sultan and would not be deposed by Egyptian fallahin, but when the sultan ratified the choice of the ulama, the governor had no option but to pack his bags and leave the country to Muhammad Ali, the new governor.

The mamluks attempted to regain their former position in the capital once the Ottoman governor had left, but they were betrayed by the ulama, who refused to allow them back to power, and they were soon to face several years of fighting with Muhammad Ali, from 1805, when he had been proclaimed governor, until 1811, when mamluk resistance ended.

The sultan had accepted the ulama's candidate as governor for the time being, but he had no intention of establishing Muhammad

Ali as a permanent governor. In any case it was Ottoman custom not to allow a governor to stay longer than a year in any one place, although there were exceptions. Muhammad Ali, an obscure Turk (although some believe he was a Kurd) from the city of Kavala, and the commander-in-chief of the Albanian forces, the despised mercenary wing of the Ottoman forces, became governor of Egypt in 1805. In spite of Ottoman plotting, he kept that position until 1848. He founded a dynasty that was to rule Egypt until 1952. and started a process of modernization and the development of a modern state system.

4   The beginning of the state system, 1805–1922

Muhammad Ali's reign in Egypt can be divided roughly into two periods. For the first few years he spent his time consolidating his rule and eliminating opposition. The second phase was spent in economic and military expansion. He and his supporters – his Turco-Albanian cohorts, local Muslim and minority tujjar – all contrived to establish a centralized authority that brought law and order, thereby reviving trade and commerce.

The new governor spent his early years either cajoling and bribing mamluk beys to join his ranks or fighting those who resisted until he became sole master in the land. This was achieved by 1811, when the last of the mamluks were invited to a ceremony at the citadel, ambushed and killed. The incident was a minor mopping-up operation and exterminated some twenty-four beys along with their lieutenants. This was an age of bloody incidents and the new wali did no more to the mamluks than they would have done to him had their positions been reversed.

By that time plans for the future of Egypt had become clearer to the new governor, and a regular programme of action was being sketched out in his mind. To begin with, Muhammad Ali and his supporters were mercantilists who believed in expanding agriculture for export, as some tujjar had done under the mamluks, but they also wished to introduce industrialization so as to benefit from the agricultural raw materials grown locally and become self-sufficient, thus preventing bullion from being exported. Fearful of foreign encroachments on Egypt (for the British had attempted an occupation of the country in 1807 and had been beaten), or of being displaced or ousted by his suzerain, the sultan, Muhammad Ali and his administration sought to strengthen the army and build a navy and a merchant marine. The first attempts at industrialization were geared towards a military-industrial complex that allowed Egypt to manufacture her own military hardware and thus end reliance on foreign imports. Everything that had been at first imported was promptly copied in the new factories, which were able to turn out rifles, muskets, cannon, gunpowder and small arms in respectable quantities.

The next step in terms of industrialization was to found textile factories and use locally grown cotton, flax and linen. By 1821 long-staple cotton had been discovered and that was also put into production. Silkworms and mulberry trees were imported from Syria and Lebanon in order to expand the production and manufacture of silk. Even cashmere goats were imported from India in an attempt to improve the production of wool.

Once industrialization was well under way it became necessary to find markets for these commodities, and a programme of military expansion along the traditional trade routes of the country followed. Initially expansion went towards the Hijaz, where the sultan had urged Muhammad Ali to go and put down a revolt of the Wahhabis against Ottoman authority. The Wahhabis, followers of a fundamentalist religious reformer, had conquered all of the areas that form modern Saudi Arabia, including the holy cities of Mecca and Medina, thereby overthrowing the yoke of the sultan, who was protector of the holy cities. Furthermore the Wahhabis had stopped the pilgrimage caravans from entering the holy cities, and thus struck at the financial well-being of the Ottoman empire as well as at its standing at the head of the Muslim community. The Ottoman sultan urged Muhammad Ali to fight the Wahhabis, hoping thereby either that the new wali·of Egypt would be defeated, and the Ottomans would be rid of a troublesome upstart, or that he would succeed and rid the sultan of a dangerous religious-political movement. In either case the Ottomans had nothing to lose by sending Muhammad Ali to fight in the Hijaz, and indeed had a great deal to gain. Muhammad Ali's armies finally put down the Wahhabi movement in 1818 (although the movement never died out, for a second Wahhabi kingdom was to rise).

Once the Hijaz campaign was over and Muhammad Ali's son Ibrahim had been appointed governor of the region, the wali turned his attention towards the Sudan. The Ottomans, fearful of their governor's military prowess, had refused to send him any mamluks or mercenaries for his depleted armies; moreover he desperately needed gold to finance his projects. He hoped to find both in the Sudan: slaves for his armies and a source of wealth. The Sudan expedition failed as far as gold and men were concerned. The gold found was of poor quality and not worth mining and the Sudanese could not adapt to the Egyptian climate or food and died like flies. However, the conquest of the Sudan added an enormous piece of territory to Egypt, which by 1822 had become an empire instead of a province among many that were subject to the Ottoman suzerain. For although the wali was still nominally a governor of a province, he controlled the Hijaz and the Sudan as well.

The army in Egypt was forced to undergo a process of transformation when it could not obtain men from the Ottoman empire or from the Sudan. In the past, armies were formed of heterogeneous ethnic groups, North Africans, Bosniaks, Mingrelians, Circassians, Albanians and others. They were groups of men who obeyed their own officers and no one else, and were paid by the same officers, and deserted when they pleased. There was no unified command, little discipline, and not even a common language. That was soon to change as the army was turned into a European-style fighting force. Muhammad Ali hired French officers, who had flocked to Egypt in search of employment once Napoleon's army had been disbanded, and they induced the ruler to try to draft Egyptian fallahin into the new army. After all, they reasoned, Napoleon had done it with French peasants; why could Muhammad Ali not do it with Egyptians? At first the ruler was appalled at the idea of fallahin becoming soldiers, but he soon saw there was no alternative and agreed to drafting Egyptians into the army. In time the Egyptian army was to number well over 100,000 men. The senior officers were all Ottoman, but the rank and file and the younger officers up to the rank of captain were Egyptians.

Not only was the army modernized and streamlined, but it was also armed with up-to-date weaponry. Modernizing an army inevitably led to developing and expanding a programme of education in terms of staff college, engineering corps, medical surgeons and veterinary surgeons. Schools were opened in Egypt and educational missions sent abroad to learn technology, not only in the field of military science but in other fields as well. Thus the army became the impetus for a wide programme of education of a new, secular nature. It was not that the new administration wished to educate Egyptians in the abstract; it was simply that they saw the necessity for importing technology, and education was the only way to do it. Muhammad Ali, who was illiterate until the age of 47, had an enthusiasm for education that verged on being a fetish. He constantly advised his sons and daughters (who numbered thirty) to study hard and to learn the 'arts and sciences', as education was the key to success and would open the future to them. The only time he showed anger towards his children was when they were reluctant to learn their lessons.

The ambitious programmes that were established in Egypt necessitated a large purse which the country, racked by years of warfare and foreign exploitation, was hard put to provide. The first capital was amassed fortuitously through the capture of stores of grain in Upper Egypt when the mamluks were defeated. The grain was exported to feed the British armies enmeshed in the Peninsular wars against Napoleon's armies from 1808 to 1812. It was sold for continually rising prices and supplied capital that was used to expand the irrigation system; that permitted two and even three crops a year in some areas in place of the traditional one. Basin irrigation was slowly being converted to a system of perennial irrigation. The newly irrigated lands were planted with crops geared towards a cash-crop economy for export; they were planted with cotton, sugar-cane, indigo and flax. This was not an entirely new departure for from the middle of the eighteenth century Egypt had been gradually shifting towards a cash-crop economy in response to European industrialization, the demand for raw materials, and as an alternative source of income occasioned by the decline in the coffee and textile trade. The new rulers accelerated that trend in their need for funds and their need to dominate the means of production more thoroughly.

Land tenure was reformed. The former tax-farmers were dispossessed by the new regime and some of the land given to the new elite. That elite was composed of the governor, his family and his retainers, as well as the native Egyptians who had been co-opted into the administration. The native Egyptian notables *(ayan)*, who had been village heads *(sheikh al-balad* or *umda)* under the mamluks, were used by the new administration and entrusted with collecting the taxes and generally representing the government at the village level. To reward the rural administrators for their new functions they were given grants of land of some five per cent out of every 105 faddans. It was from among the group of rural notables, the ayan, that local landowners were created, and by the end of the century their holdings were to develop into large latifundia.

Changes in land tenure were necessary to bring about changes in agricultural output from the level of a subsistence economy to a cash-crop economy. The fallah was strictly regimented. In the past he had been left to his own devices, and had worked roughly 150 days a year. The rest of the year the land lay fallow under flood waters, and the fallah occupied himself with cottage industries, supplementing his income, or remained idle if he so wished. Under the new regime he was told what to plant, when to plant it, and he had to sell it to the government at fixed prices. These prices may have been higher than the amounts he had made in an earlier age, but the fallah was more exploited by virtue of the extra man-hours he was now forced to work in planting the new crops, and in the high degree of regimentation he had to endure. The fallah was made to work 250 days a year on irrigated land if it were planted with new, labour-intensive crops such as cotton or sugar-cane. He was dragooned into corvée labour to dig out new ditches and canals and clean out the old ditches, which periodically had to be deepened and cleaned of an accumulation of silt. This function was made worse when the fallah was expected to provide corvée labour on the lands of the high and the mighty as well. It is true that in the past he had also provided corvée labour on the lands of the mamluks and tax-farmers, where he had been treated, in the words of a chronicler, worse than a slave, but the working period had been of shorter duration. Corvée labour now disrupted family life, for the fallah was sometimes taken to dig a canal in another part of the country and his family, who had no other means of support, was obliged to follow him. The administration claimed that, contrary to past custom, it paid and fed corvée workers, which was certainly true in most cases; nevertheless corvée imposed an extra hardship on the fallah, whether he was paid or not, for he did not have a free choice.

New land brought under cultivation through irrigation projects was offered to anyone who wished to work it. Land taxes were remitted for a number of years until the land had yielded a crop. In its search for manpower the administration tried to settle bedouin tribes and make peasants out of them. It successfully wooed tribal chiefs by granting them tribal lands free of taxation on condition that the bedouin tilled the soil. Tribal chiefs soon became latifundists. Any fallah who guaranteed to pay the tax on land was allowed to take over land. The problem at the time was not lack of land but lack of manpower.

The programme of industrialization that was introduced into the country exacerbated the manpower shortage. Even were we to assume that men used in the new factories were not of fallah origin but were urban workers who had been turned into a proletariat through the events of the last century and the decline in artisan production, industrialization did use up a certain percentage of manpower. When the army was expanded and incorporated Egyptian ranks that problem was to worsen; fallahin were forcibly removed from the soil and drafted into the army.

The army became the most unpopular form of employment. While the factories were disliked, the army was feared. Conscripts sometimes tried to maim themselves to avoid conscription, which was carried out in as brutal a manner as was then the practice in

Europe, and by the same methods. Muhammad Ali and his government involved Egypt in a number of wars: the Hijaz (1811–18), the Sudan (1820–2), Crete, Cyprus and the Morea (1824–8) and finally two wars in Syria (1831–3 and 1839–40). All of these wars, save that in the Hijaz, were fought with conscripts from among a population that at most numbered five million people. And yet the army became a major instrument of Egyptianization, for, so long as aliens manned the army, Egyptians could not call their land their own.

Ibrahim Pasha, Muhammad Ali's eldest son and commander-in-chief, wanted to Egyptianize the entire army and promote Egyptians to the highest military ranks. In his youth, at the age of sixteen, he had been sent to Istanbul as a hostage for his father's good behaviour and as a guarantee that the money his father had promised to pay the imperial treasury in return for being maintained governor of Egypt would be paid. That year spent in exile in Istanbul marked Ibrahim and turned him against the Ottomans. In later years he used to say that he had arrived in Egypt a young boy and the hot sun of Egypt had baked him into an Egyptian. He remembered no other homeland and felt loyalty to no other entity than to Egypt, and certainly not to the Ottomans whom he disliked and despised. Unlike his father who, even when he went to war against the Ottomans, still considered himself an Ottoman, Ibrahim was an Egyptian. Much like the American colonists who had fought a war of independence, Muhammad Ali wanted economic and military independence from the Ottomans, but wanted to maintain his cultural links. Ibrahim on the other hand wanted independence utterly and completely. He harassed his father until he was allowed to promote Egyptians to the ranks of captain and major, and assured him that they were more loyal to his family and country than ever were the Turks who served in their army.

Not only the army but also the administration was Egyptianized. Officials from the post of sub-governor of a province downwards were now all native Egyptians. Only governors of provinces remained Ottomans and that was to change by the next generation. For the first time Egyptians became an active part of the administration and were not merely relegated to the position of book-keepers and scribes, the traditional fiefs of the Coptic community. Whether they were Egyptian or Ottoman, the officials in the administration were constantly harassed by the ruler and enjoined to perform better, to treat the population kindly, to be honest and diligent. Some of these homilies fell on deaf ears. They were followed by letters beginning with 'Donkey' or worse, 'Pig son of a pig', and ending with threats to pluck out their beards, hair by hair, to throw them into the sea or river alive, to have them buried or, the final ignominy, to have them broken to the ranks of the fallahin, presumably a fate worse than death, especially to an Ottoman. The administration was kept on its collective toes by chiding, threats and promises of reward. Slowly but surely the country was pushed and pulled into taking the form of a state.

In most countries feelings of kinship among the population create the need for a state; in Egypt it was the other way round. The state first came into existence and then roused feelings of kinship and belonging among the population. Muhammad Ali created a state out of a former Ottoman province, and gave Egyptians a sense of identity and a stake in the state by dragooning them into government. The state allowed Egyptians, for the first time since the pharaohs, to identify in some measure with the administration – but complete identification was only to come a century later. The administration was manned by Egyptians, albeit in a minor capacity, although their numbers were soon to grow and engulf the aliens.

The wars that were to occupy the administration for so many years arose as a consequence of the mercantilist economic planning which had developed in Europe. That a country needed to export more than it imported was one of the basic principles of such thought. In consequence import substitution was established and local materials fabricated for export. However, in order to push forward an aggressive export policy, the easiest path to take was conquest and the creation of colonies that became markets for the new industries. Furthermore the newly occupied colonies would provide further raw materials for industry, and expertise and manpower for industry and the army. Should the colonies also border the Mediterranean, they would give Egypt control over the eastern part of the Sea and therefore control over the commerce of that region. Expansion therefore logically followed the trade routes, the Hijaz, the Sudan, the Morea and Syria.

The Morean campaign was embarked upon at the invitation, or rather at the command, of the sultan. The Greek war of independence had shown the Ottomans that their army was no match for those they had called a 'rabble'. They were obliged to turn to Muhammad Ali, the most powerful governor in the empire. In true Ottoman fashion they were afraid to send his army to the Morea, in case it turned on the imperial capital itself, and so wasted time sending his forces off to conquer Crete and Cyprus, which was promptly done. By then the Ottomans had no recourse but to send the Egyptian army under the leadership of Ibrahim, Muhammad Ali's son, into the Morea, promising the wali that province and Syria as his reward for success.

Ibrahim Pasha was successful in bringing the province under his control, in fact too successful and so gave the European Powers cause for worry. The Russians were in two minds about the Greeks; much as they wished for a Greek vassal state they also feared the consequences of a war of independence which might in the future turn Greece into a haven for revolutionaries with like intentions. On the other hand the Greeks feared Russian influence over them and turned to England for assistance. England wished for an independent Greece, for British merchants had been involved with Greek merchants in trade for some time and together they had dominated trade in the Black Sea area, if not the eastern Mediterranean. At the same time the British were fearful of Russian ascendancy in the Mediterranean, which to all intents and purposes had become a British lake once Napoleon's navy had been destroyed.

Common cause with a Christian people against the hated Muslim Ottomans drove other European countries to join in the move against Ibrahim in the Morea. That occupation was presented to the European public by the press as a move on the part of Muslims

to exterminate Christians. Rumours were spread of wholesale depor-
tations of the Greek population, and of horrendous acts of barbarism
carried out by Ibrahim's army, most of which were patently untrue.
Barbarism was not limited to one army, for the Greeks were as bar-
baric as the Egyptian army, and indeed as any other European army of
the day. Posing as humanitarians, but motivated by the same greed
that animated all other contenders in the fray – except perhaps the
Greeks themselves, who at least were fighting for their independence
– an Anglo-Franco-Austrian fleet sank the combined Ottoman-
Egyptian fleet in 1827 in the Bay of Navarino. The army under
Ibrahim's command was stranded in the Morea without hope of supplies or food reaching it, for the European navy promptly imposed a
blockade. Finally Muhammad Ali was forced to arrange for the withdrawal of his army from the Morea on board European ships on condition that his army evacuate the region.

The Morean campaign had cost the wali a great deal of money
and had brought little reward, for when the wali asked for Syria he
was soundly rebuffed. He planned to occupy Syria anyway and over
the next two years prepared for the invasion of that country. This was
carried out very rapidly. Time and again the Ottoman armies were
defeated by the newly trained Egyptian army, until the Ottoman
prime minister was captured in battle. The prince of Lebanon became
an ally of the Egyptians and opened up the Lebanon to their armies.
In 1833 the Ottomans finally conceded defeat when the Egyptians
came to within marching distance of the capital; they were forced to
grant the region of southern Anatolia and greater Syria as provinces
to be governed by Ibrahim Pasha.

Such a victory was not to go unpunished. The Ottomans had
appealed to the British for help, but the British government was otherwise occupied with European crises, five of which threatened to
develop into major conflagrations, so they had little time to spare for
the Ottomans. On the other hand, once the Egyptian armies had come
to within a day's march of the capital, the Russians rushed to the aid
of their traditional enemies, the Ottomans, and offered to sign a treaty

with them. The treaty signed in Unkiar Skelessi in 1833 contained a secret clause which promised to keep the Dardanelles open to Russian shipping in time of war and close it to all other shipping. That treaty granted Russia the one constant demand in Russian foreign policy from the time of Catherine the Great to the present, the need for the Russian fleet to have access to a warm sea and to acquire a footing in the Mediterranean. Once Russian armies became stationed on the other side of the Bosphorus, Ibrahim's armies could advance no further and the peace of Kutahia was signed between the Ottomans and the Egyptians in 1833.

When the British government learned the terms of the Treaty of Unkiar Skelessi they were incensed, especially Palmerston, the foreign secretary for most of the period. Palmerston was further exercised by Muhammad Ali's aggressive industrial policies, which were becoming bothersome to British merchants. In his bid to control the country's resources the wali controlled all imports and exports. Only selected merchants, among whom was Samuel Briggs, an Englishman, were allowed to buy and sell in the country, and they had to buy from and sell to the wali, who thus became the sole merchant. He placed embargoes on imported materials which rivalled Egyptian products, believing this to be a necessary measure to protect his infant industries until they became competitive. Trade substitution and embargoes went hand in hand. British textiles which had been dumped in Egypt and had ruined a number of textile factories were embargoed. Long-staple cotton, prized by English textile makers and grown in Egypt from 1821, was beginning to be used in Egyptian factories, which caused the industrialists to fear that in time it would all be used up locally. Such policies conflicted with the free trade movement, which was sweeping over England precisely because it suited the British economy, which sought to impose free trade on other countries, by force if necessary – as in the opium wars in China – but held on to a protective tariff at home as far as corn was concerned.

Expansion into Syria ran counter to British commercial interests, for the Middle East had become a major market for British goods.

In the 1830s Britain was going through a tremendous economic crisis, and set up an aggressive export policy that was necessary to save British industry. This policy was supported by the British government, especially by Palmerston, to enable British industrialists to live off 'shirts for brown men and black men'. That policy ran counter to Muhammad Ali's interests, who, once in occupation of Syria, tried to dump Egyptian goods, rather than British ones there, and sought to exploit Syrian resources for Egyptian ends. British commercial interests were shaken by a policy that threatened to close off the eastern Mediterranean market to British goods, even though in fact it did not do so and British trade increased rather than diminished during that period. Palmerston consequently turned to the Ottoman sultan and assured him of British assistance against his tiresome vassal. A commercial treaty was signed between the Ottoman empire and Britain in 1838, the treaty of Balta Liman. That treaty set import and export tariffs that favoured British and all other European merchants at the expense of the local merchants, who were stuck with higher tariffs. The British official who negotiated the treaty led the Ottomans to believe that, because the treaty specified an end to all monopolies, it would destroy Muhammad Ali's economic base and so weaken his ability to finance his armies. At the same time the same official was perfectly conscious that the treaty would also ruin the Ottoman economy, but the Ottomans were not informed of that one detail.

Before the terms of the treaty could be applied in Egypt another round of fighting broke out between the Ottoman and Egyptian armies when the Ottomans attacked Egyptian positions in Syria. Once again the Ottomans were defeated by Ibrahim's troops in the battle of Nezib in 1840. This time the British government stepped in and prevented the Ottomans from surrendering to Egyptian terms. They convinced the rest of Europe – including the French who had been allies of Muhammad Ali – to support its *démarche* against Ibrahim in Syria. Troops were landed in Beirut, and Ibrahim not only had to try to smother a flare of uprisings all over Syria which had been incited by British and Ottoman propaganda as well as by general dissatisfaction at being occupied; he also had to fight European forces. When the British navy paraded outside his bedroom window in Alexandria, Muhammad Ali admitted defeat, and he was forced to withdraw his army from Syria.

The wali's grand design came to nought, thanks to British interference. He was forced to be content with the hereditary pashalik of Egypt, succession going by Ottoman law to the oldest male member of the ruling family, and to abide by the Treaty of London of 1840. The terms of the Treaty of Balta Liman were applied to Egypt; the wali resisted them for a while, but eventually had to submit. His embargoes and monopolies were disbanded, as were those of his industries which dealt with weapons and war-related commodities. The rest of the factories, divested of protection, were soon clearly shown to be no match for cheaper European goods which benefited from tariff advantages written into the Treaty of Balta Liman. The experiment at industrialization was suspended for a century. Egypt was relegated to the status of a province, whose sole commercial and economic function was to supply raw materials for European industry. From having become the centre of an empire, it was once again broken to the ranks of a mere province.

Some historians would have us believe that Muhammad Ali's reign cost Egypt a great deal in terms of money, lives lost and a wasted attempt at industrialization that was doomed to fail. But Muhammad Ali Egyptianized Egypt, although he himself did not plan to do that and never knew that he had done it. He had also established a state formation and an administration that followed logical principles of government. He had given the Egyptian fallah, who fought in his armies, a sense of pride at having beaten the Ottomans, and a sense of achievement that went a long way to giving him a positive self-identity even though he hated the army and sought to get out of conscription. The wali had established schools for science and technology; he had introduced hundreds of plants, trees and varieties of fruit, so that today almost all the fruit and vegetables of Egypt date from that time. He had continued economic trends that had appeared in the eighteenth century, which geared the economy towards export to the European market. In this I believe he had little choice; sooner or later Egypt and the entire Ottoman empire would have become engulfed in the European market system and would have lost their local, autonomous markets, bowing to European domination and demand. Such domination accelerated changes in land tenure, which caused the fallah to become landless, alienated him from his tools of production and away from a subsistence economy, in order to direct land towards the production of cash crops and an export-oriented economy.

Muhammad Ali had tried to wrest more rights for his successors from the Ottomans, but he knew that his successors would have a difficult time. Ibrahim, a capable and energetic man, had contracted tuberculosis and died before his father, while the rest of his family were either children or indolent and reactionary, like Abbas, the wali's grandson. The wali's own health was undermined by a dose of silver nitrate administered by his physicians, who hoped to cure his dysentery; this caused massive brain damage, so that he lapsed into bouts of madness alternating with bouts of lucidity. When the latter became less frequent he was replaced (in 1848) as head of government by his son Ibrahim, without being conscious of the fact. Ibrahim died a few months later and was succeeded by Abbas. Muhammad Ali finally died in 1849.

Unfortunately for Egypt none of Muhammad Ali's successors had half his energy or imagination, to say nothing of his political skill. Abbas wanted a return to the Ottoman fold, and concentrated his energies on extracting as much from agriculture as he could. He radically diminished the size of the army and navy – not only because the terms of the agreement with the Ottomans so dictated, but because he wished to economize and saw no advantage to having an army or a navy. He considered industrialization a waste of money for he himself made vast profits out of selling raw materials from his extensive estates. The only bright economic spot in his reign was the railway line that went from Cairo to Suez and made life easier for travellers of the Peninsular and Orient Steamship Line. His reign ended in 1854 when some of his companions assassinated him. He was succeeded by his uncle, Muhammad Ali's son, Said.

Said was a corpulent man whose childhood had been made sheer misery by his father nagging him to lose weight. Muhammad Ali's disgust at corpulence caused him to send weekly letters to his son demanding that he lose weight, expressing displeasure at his flabby appearance, putting him on a strict regimen, or suggesting more and more tiring exercises to help him lose weight. Said, who served in the navy, was ordered to climb up and down the ship's masts several times a day, to run up and down the palace staircase or round the walls of Alexandria. The fat, insecure child, who never lost his flab, was befriended by the French consul Ferdinand de Lesseps, who, it was rumoured, also fed him with plates of spaghetti in secret. A bond was forged between the two men and, later on, Said was easily convinced that all he had to do to make his name famous throughout the world was to sign the concession offered by his friend, to build a canal at Suez that would unite the Mediterranean and the Red Sea. Though Said by so doing did become famous it was more for his gullibility in signing an unfavourable concession, one which eventually necessitated negotiating a foreign loan to pay for those shares that remained unsold which he never wanted but de Lesseps foisted onto him. The canal was to cause the death of 100,000 Egyptians who had to dig it as corvée labour, using their bare hands, since the company refused to provide the workers with either tools or even food and shelter. 60,000 Egyptians were mobilized to dig the canal in three shifts of 20,000 workers, thus denying their services to agriculture.

The whole scheme was highly irregular, as Said had no legal authority to initiate such a project without the approval of the Ottoman sultan. When the sultan refused to grant approval de Lesseps defiantly went on with the project. He hoped his cousin, the Empress Eugénie, would bring pressure to bear on the sultan to allow the project to go forward unhindered. There were well founded rumours that the prime minister of France and the Empress had both received secret shares in the project. The British railway lobby meanwhile had killed the project in England, for it would compete unfavourably with their railways in Egypt. The British government bullied the sultan into refusing to give his consent to the concession, while the French tried to bully or cajole him by turns into giving his consent. By the time consent was given the canal was almost half finished.

Said was supposed to be succeeded by his nephew Ahmad, Ibrahim Pasha's eldest son, but Ahmad had died in a railway accident. Ahmad and a group of princes had been inaugurating a new railway line that spanned the Nile over a swing bridge. Someone forgot to close the bridge on time and the entire train hurtled into the Nile killing all on board except for Prince Halim, Muhammad Ali's youngest son, who was sitting near an open window and swam out of the wreckage. Ismail, Ahmad's younger brother, was the only prince who had not attended the festivities, claiming an indisposition, and so he became the ruler of Egypt. Ahmad's family have always suspected Ismail of having had a hand in arranging the incident, but there has been no evidence to sustain that suspicion.

Ismail (1863–79) had a reputation as a canny gentleman farmer whose lands were a model estate. On first reaching the throne he had to borrow money to pay off further debts incurred by the canal. The Suez Canal Company claimed the Egyptian government owed it funds and both parties decided on arbitration, with the arbiter being Napoleon III. This was setting the cat among the pigeons, for Napoleon III decided the Egyptian government should pay damages to the Suez Canal Company for land to which the company had no legal right. Furthermore the price of such land was estimated at some future rate when the land, which at the moment of arbitration was desert, had been watered and turned into cultivable land. Furthermore the Egyptian government was to dig a canal bringing water from the Nile to the new canal cities. The sweet-water canal was to irrigate the desert and render it cultivable, and the water of that canal was to be sold back to the Egyptian government by the canal company. Such an outrageous arbitration decision netted the canal company the exact amount they needed in order to finish the canal.

Ismail, who had grandiose ideas for Egypt, wanted to gain the good graces of Napoleon and did not protest at the arbitration decision. His various projects soon forced him to borrow more money from European banks. He expanded irrigation canals and brought further land under the perennial system of irrigation so land produced two and three crops. One of these crops was cotton and for a while Egypt benefited from the cotton boom caused by the Civil War in the United States. Unfortunately the boom came to a rapid halt when the war ended and the price of cotton plummeted, ruining a number of fallahin who had planned on continuing high prices. A cattle murrain the following year carried off the entire livestock of the country, which had to be replaced by importing new beasts from abroad. Further projects followed: harbours were deepened and widened, lighthouses built, roads paved, bridges built. The country was provided with an infrastructure of roads and railway lines which speeded the export of raw materials, the country's basic wealth.

In 1869 the Suez Canal was inaugurated with maximum pomp. The crowned heads of Europe, including the Empress Eugénie, the Crown Prince of Prussia and assorted minor royalty, were invited to the ceremonies. Ismail fancied himself a member of that select club of royals and put himself and his country out to show what luxury and expenditure they were capable of producing. Cities were supplied with street lighting for the occasion, and palaces were built in the new cities of Port Said and Ismailiyya. An opera house graced Cairo and Verdi was commissioned to write an opera on an ancient Egyptian theme supplied by Auguste Mariette, the famous Egyptologist. Unfortunately the costumes were not ready on time and on the opening night *Rigoletto* was performed instead of *Aida*.

Ismail tried to get the Ottomans to declare Egypt independent by bribing officials, but with no success. He did however get them to recognize him as Khedive, a Persian word meaning ruler, a title which his grandfather had unofficially used. The new title was meant to differentiate between his position and that of the other Ottoman governors of provinces who did not possess the same degree of autonomy. The sultan, who was Ismail's first cousin (their mothers being sisters), did allow him to change the law of succession to one of primogeniture in return for doubling the tribute to the Porte (the Ottoman imperial government). All the reforms instituted by Ismail, extravagant though they were, aimed at building the productive capacity of the country, but they also cost a great deal of money which the country could not supply. Without an infrastructure the rationalization of agriculture for export would not have been as successful, for the new railway lines went all over the delta to carry cotton to the ports or to bring grain from Upper Egypt. Having borrowed beyond his country's means, Ismail soon found himself unable to pay even the interest on his debts, which increased with every new loan negotiated. To help him find a solution to his financial difficulties, in 1866 Ismail called the first parliament. This was supposed to be a purely consultative body and to meet at least twice every year. Clearly that body was designed to help the ruler raise more taxes from the population and not to advise him in any other fashion. The delegates were all landowners with a stake in the agricultural well-being of the country and, while that parliament had no teeth, successive parliaments soon developed a life of their own.

In desperation, Ismail turned to the European Powers to help him out of his financial morass, and by so doing he took a fatal step that allowed the Powers from then on to interfere actively in internal Egyptian affairs. In 1876 an institution known as the Caisse de la Dette Publique was set up. That body was composed of four commissioners representing the chief bondholding countries, England, France, Austria and Italy. Two controllers, one English and one French, were appointed to supervise state revenue and expenditure, hence the name of Dual Control by which the system came to be known. The controllers were appointed by the Khedive and could be dismissed by him.

These measures did not prove sufficient and the Powers urged Ismail to hand over the reins of government to a ministry containing two European members, an Englishman and a Frenchman, who controlled income and expenditure. The European ministers, in an attempt at economic retrenchment, cashiered army officers. The army officers mutinied and manhandled the two foreign ministers, giving Ismail – who had probably fomented the whole incident to show that only he controlled the country – the excuse to dismiss the cabinet. By then the Powers were becoming worried their bondholders, those with shares in the debt, would not get paid the interest on their loans and the country would default on payment.

By 1879 the controllers found there was no money to pay the interest due on the debt and suggested the country take measures which were tantamount to a declaration of bankruptcy. Ismail refused and put forward an alternative plan of his own, with the help of the parliament, but the controllers refused the plan and resigned. The British controller, Sir Evelyn Baring, a member of the banking family that owned a sizeable proportion of the debt, put pressure on his government to get Ismail deposed, which was accomplished in 1879. It is interesting to note that years later when Baring became British Consul-General and Agent in Egypt (the uncrowned ruler of the country) he brought Egypt to solvency by following the same plan Ismail had proposed and he had turned down as unfeasible.

Ismail, who had been a strong and autocratic ruler, was deposed with the minimum of fuss on the part of his subjects, who blamed him for their financial woes, and who hated his autocracy. He was succeeded by his son Tawfiq (1879–92), who had neither his father's qualities nor abilities, and fell entirely under the domination of the European consuls. In 1880 he negotiated the Law of Liquidation with the Powers. By that agreement Egypt's revenue was estimated at an inflated £9 million and divided into two unequal parts, the larger going to the Caisse de la Dette to pay off the bondholders, and the smaller to defray the expenses of the administration. Out of its share of funds the government was supposed to pay the tribute to the Porte and to make up any deficits the Caisse might incur. That law effected a stranglehold on Egypt, which from that moment on was unable to move without European permission.

When Ismail had been short of funds he had been induced to sell his shares in the Suez Canal and was finally ordered to sell his preferential shares, the only source of income from the Canal that was left to the country. Such a move made no sense in economic terms, but it did make a lot of sense in political terms, for those who had advised the sale made sure the shares were bought by the British government, with a loan from the Rothschild Bank, for £4 million. These were the famous shares that Disraeli claimed gave England control of the canal and, while the shares did nothing of the kind, they were the thin end of the wedge, because Britain negotiated to have two members sit on the board of the company.

Worse than the loss of the Suez Canal shares was the increasing power granted to aliens as a result of the capitulations. The capitulations were grants of extraterritoriality given by Ottoman sultans from the sixteenth century to various European Powers, along with the right to trade in Ottoman territories. The grants allowed Europeans to station in the Ottoman empire consuls who would try any of their citizens who resided in the area for the infringement of their own national law. (According to Ottoman custom, Ottoman Muslim law was applicable only to Muslims; religious minorities were tried by their own church hierarchy.) As the Ottoman empire weakened and became unable to defend itself against European military and economic encroachments, the capitulations were abused by the Europeans, who used them as a means of avoiding both taxation and the law. With the complicity of their consuls, Europeans in the empire could commit any crime with impunity. Their punishment was to be shipped out, but they could return on the next ship and local authorities could do nothing about it. Smuggling therefore flourished. Alien residents paid no taxes, even though they controlled most of the sources of wealth, and the burden of taxation therefore fell on the hapless fallah. Moneylenders did a thriving trade by lending the fallah money at usurious rates, which rose as high as 20 per cent a month, and when the fallah could not pay the interest on the debt his land was seized for non-payment. Along with the national debt, the indebtedness of the fallahin was another calamity to befall the country.

During the last years of Ismail's reign a number of rich landowners had been pushing for a constitutional form of government which would protect them from their ruler's arbitrariness and guarantee them a say in government. The advent of Tawfiq to power had encouraged these pashas to believe that a new form of government might be in the offing. Many of these rich landowners, who also held the Ottoman/Egyptian title of pasha, were members of a Masonic lodge, as were Tawfiq and a remarkable activist, Sayyid Jamal al-Din al-Afghani. Al-Afghani had travelled all over the Middle East rousing people to political activity, and preaching religious reform and liberal political ideas. In Egypt he encouraged the rise of a constitutional movement and got a younger generation of intellectuals to found newspapers and preach liberal ideas. Thus, when Tawfiq came to power and got a constitutional supporter, Sharif Pasha, to draw up a constitution and then appointed him premier, all these men assumed their ideas regarding government would prevail. Under the influence of the British consul, Tawfiq soon changed his mind and had al-Afghani arrested secretly at night and deported (in his nightshirt), sacked his new premier and in his place appointed an old-fashioned premier, Riaz Pasha.

From then on we see opposition groups in the making. Three of these groups eventually came together to form a nationalist revolt. The groups were formed of the liberal pashas who wanted a constitution that would safeguard their own vested interests, their private property, and allow them a share in government along with the landowning bourgeoisie. While these pashas were autocrats in their own right and acted as such towards their peasantry, they wanted to limit the autocracy of the ruler, which is why they were referred to as liberals even though their liberalism was of a limited nature. The second group of opponents were the young intellectuals who wanted a constitution as a means of limiting autocracy in general, whether on the part of the ruler, the government or the rich landowners. They had few or no vested interests, other than the fact that many among them came from fallah stock and chafed under the tyranny of those above them. The third current was to come from the army and was motivated by entirely different reasons.

There were only four native Egyptian colonels in the army, the rest being Turco-Circassian. The Egyptians had risen from the ranks until they had reached the rank of colonel under the rule of Said. Tawfiq's minister of war, an old-fashioned Circassian, wished to limit years of service in the army to seven, so no Egyptian could rise from the ranks to become an officer and the officer corps would be strictly limited to Turco-Circassians graduating from the military schools. Displeased with that ruling, the Egyptian colonels sought a show-down with the government, but rather than listen to their arguments the minister arrested the leader of the movement, a colonel named Ahmad Urabi. The colonel was released by his regiment, who had suspected a trap of some kind. That incident brought the colonels, especially Urabi, to the forefront of the Egyptian political scene as possible candidates for leadership of the opposition movement to the government. Little by little a movement had grown up in the country with a slogan 'Egypt for the Egyptians' to describe the feelings of animosity on the part of the population at the increasing control Europeans were acquiring over their country. They blamed the loss of control on the government and their spineless ruler. Opposition gathered round Urabi and his companions, who had a second showdown with the Khedive in front of the palace. Speaking in the 'name of the people' and surrounded by their regiments, the colonels demanded a constitution, a change of government and an increase in the size of the army to the 18,000 men specified in the Treaty of London in 1840.

The Khedive tried to get the Ottomans or the British to send him troops to quell the mutiny, but to the Egyptians he pretended to go along with these demands. Once again Sharif Pasha was appointed premier and summoned a constituent assembly. In January 1881

France and England sent a Joint Note, which stated that as far as the two countries were concerned the Khedive was the only guarantee of good order and the development of prosperity in Egypt. The Khedive from then on assumed he need not cooperate with his new regime and so intrigued against them. The rest of the country viewed the Note as a threat of an impending invasion by the Powers, and so threw their lot in with the army as the sole instrument to protect them from invasion. For the next few months the stage was set for a final confrontation between the Khedive and his subjects. Rumours flew that the Khedive was to be deposed by the Urabists, that Halim, Muhammad Ali's youngest son, was to become the new Khedive. The consuls added fuel to the fire of the rumours by claiming that the country was in the grip of anarchy, when in fact it was under the control of the army. The men on the spot, the British consul, the Controller and others, induced the British cabinet to believe the Urabists were dangerous revolutionaries who were out to take over government and had to be destroyed by military means.

Once again the British and French governments decided on action and sent a joint fleet to parade to the west of the city of Alexandria, where the Khedive had retired during the summer months. The presence of the fleet made the population nervous and the aliens resident in the city began to arm for the day when the natives would rise and massacre them. Eventually an incident occurred when a Greek man who was drunk stabbed an Arab donkey boy who had asked for his fare. People assumed the massacre had begun and fired from their windows at the passers-by. Generalized hysteria swept the city. Urabi, who had been appointed minister of war and entrusted with public security, was in Cairo at the time and was not informed of the events until the afternoon. He immediately left for Alexandria and quelled the riots. By then numbers of Egyptians and foreigners had been killed, the city was looted and parts were set on fire. The Khedive, who was in secret communication with the allied fleet, suggested the ships bombard the city and land marines to save his throne from the revolutionaries. The French refused to go along with a bombardment and withdrew, while the British admiral, Sir Beauchamp Seymour, took the Khedive's advice and, using a trumped-up charge that the Egyptians were fortifying forts on the other side of the harbour to the east of the city, bombarded the city. The Khedive, presiding over a council of ministers, counselled his army to resist the British to the last man. Once the bombardment began the Khedive promptly declared Urabi a rebel, divested him of his functions and sought refuge on a British man-of-war. Urabi declared the Khedive a traitor and rallied the army to resist a British invasion.

British forces landed in Alexandria while a second group sailed down the Suez Canal and landed in Ismailiyya catching the Egyptian army in a pincer movement. A battle between both armies ended in defeat for the Egyptians at Tal al-Kabir. One of the few funny stories that came out of that whole sordid incident was that the Egyptians had seen the tents of the British army at a distance and had detected what looked like people wearing skirts. They assumed the British army had brought their women with them and determined to kidnap them at night in order to demoralize the army. The skirted people were in fact the men of the Gordon Highlanders wearing kilts. When the Egyptians attempted to kidnap them at night they received a rude shock at the ferocity of the resistance with which they were met. They returned to their camp wondering how the men of the British army would fight if their women fought so fiercely. Ahmad Urabi left the battlefield before the battle was over, took the train to Cairo, and surrendered to the head of the British forces.

The Khedive had invited the British army to occupy his country in order to restore his authority; he expected this to be carried out expeditiously, after which the British forces would then evacuate the country. The British occupation of Egypt was to last until 1954.

Urabi and his companions were tried on charges of mutiny and sentenced to death, though the sentence was commuted to life imprisonment in exile in the Seychelles. Meanwhile Lord Dufferin was sent to Egypt to investigate for the British government what they were to do with a country they had occupied in what they thought was a brief 'rescue and retire' mission. Dufferin produced a marvellous document of casuistry which called for a puppet parliament with no powers, and for a British presence to supervise reforms that were deemed necessary for the well-being of the country and to make sure the bondholders continued to be paid. The main interest the British had in Egypt, apart from the bondholders, was the Suez Canal, which by then had become the lifeline to their possessions in India.

Sir Evelyn Baring returned to Egypt as Her Britannic Majesty's Consul-General and Agent. He approved of the Dufferin report but insisted that reforms necessitated a long occupation of Egypt, for, according to him, the Egyptian administration was hopelessly incompetent. Much later when the Egyptians had learnt to rule themselves, the British forces might see fit to evacuate Egypt. Baring had come to Egypt after service in India, where, as the viceroy's assistant, he had been known as vice-viceroy and as Over-Baring. In Egypt he established a principle which became known as the Granville Doctrine, after the foreign secretary of the day. That principle stated that any Egyptian minister who refused to obey Baring's directives, or those of any other British employee, would have to resign his office. British advisers were installed in key ministries and a system which came to be known as the Veiled Protectorate was established. The Veiled Protectorate meant the British in Egypt were to be the real rulers, but were not to be responsible to anyone but the British government. They were to rule from behind a façade of Egyptian ministers who had little authority, and were rubber stamps for their British manipulators.

The Khedive fully acquiesced in the system and, since he was utterly pusillanimous, was content to obey Baring in all matters. The rest of the country was cowed by a foreign occupation which had disbanded the entire Egyptian army, leaving them at the mercy of the British army. Shocked at the failure of a national revolt that ended in prison and exile for the former leaders of the revolution and for such religious intellectuals as Sheikh Muhammad Abdu, the population was subdued. The pashas who had formerly espoused the constitutionalist movement as a means of halting autocracy, hurried to show loyalty to the Khedive and to the British in Egypt; fearful of losing their possessions and suffering the Khedive's vengeance, they appealed to Baring, who protected them and exacted cooperation from them. The fallahin and rural landowners who had joined the revolution in the hope it would alleviate their indebtedness or cancel their debts soon found that they were to be laden with an extra burden, that of damages for the incidents in Alexandria, plus paying for the cost of the occupation of their country.

Baring's primary concern in Egypt was to make sure Egyptian finances were restored to solvency so no foreign power could find an excuse for interfering in Egyptian affairs through its seat on the Caisse. To that end he sought to keep the French at bay. This, together with the unilateral occupation of Egypt by the British, piqued the French into following a pinprick policy that opposed any British project and harried British actions through the Caisse, which continued to exercise influence over Egyptian finances until the debt was entirely paid off.

For the next ten years the nationalist movement showed no signs of life, as many Egyptians believed British promises of their intention to 'rescue and retire', and waited to see democratic institutions set up. None were, of course, for Baring believed that 'subject races' were totally incapable of self-government, that in fact they did not really want or need self-government, and that what they really needed was a 'full belly' policy which fed the population, kept it quiescent and allowed the elite to make money and so cooperate with the occupying power. Under the rule of Tawfiq, Baring had his way, and was the uncrowned king of Egypt. He restored Egyptian finances to solvency and helped establish British control over every ministry. The presence of the British army of occupation was a guarantee that no uprising could take place.

The Sudan, which had been conquered by Muhammad Ali, had undergone a revolution of its own at the same time that Egypt was

involved in revolution. The Sudanese revolt centred round a chilias-
tic movement, headed by a man calling himself the Mahdi, the
'Rightly Guided', who in Muslim popular eschatology was due to
appear by the end of a Muslim century and herald the end of the world
and the Last Judgement. The Egyptians were too enmeshed in their
own troubles to do anything about the Mahdi, and by the time they
were ready to take action, in 1882–3, the regular army had been disbanded. A motley crew was finally gathered under a British ex-Indian
Army officer, Hicks Pasha, who was sent to the Sudan and was massacred at the battle of Shaikan. Baring forbade any further ventures,
saying the Sudan was a bottomless hole in terms of expenditure and
he would not permit funds for its reconquest. The opposition to
Baring over the Sudan was what called forth the Granville Doctrine;
the Egyptian premier was forced to resign and the Sudan was left to
its own devices. In 1884 an eccentric Englishman, General Gordon,
who had previously seen service in the Sudan under the Khedive
Ismail, was sent to evacuate the trapped Egyptian garrisons. Gordon
decided to reconquer the Sudan instead of evacuating it and was killed
in Khartoum by the Mahdi's forces in 1885. Baring believed the Mahdi
would 'keep the bed warm' and whenever he felt ready to reconquer
the Sudan it could be done. Reconquest of the Sudan was eventually
carried out under the command of General Kitchener in 1898 and a
condominium agreement between Egypt and Britain established a
joint government. The joint government was in name only for the real
government was carried out by British officials although paid for by
the Egyptian government.

The Khedive Tawfiq died in 1892 and was replaced by his
sixteen-year-old son Abbas Hilmi (1892–1914) who had been educated
at the Theresianum in Vienna. Abbas II believed he was perfectly
capable of ruling as well as reigning and did not need a British mentor
hovering over him. By then Baring had been made Lord Cromer and,
though he had been offered ambassadorships elsewhere, he had preferred to remain in Egypt where his influence was paramount. When
the new Khedive tried to show his independence from Cromer he was

threatened with deposition if he did not obey orders; fear of deposition led the Khedive to finance and encourage an opposition movement to the British presence in Egypt among young nationalists.

The Egyptians had by then recovered from the trauma of a foreign occupation and had seen that promises of immediate evacuation were hollow. A movement aiming at ridding Egypt of the British presence was started by young nationalists led by an eighteen-year-old student named Mustafa Kamil, a gifted orator; he was soon to become a famous patriot. The nationalists and the Khedive reasoned that the British had no legal right to be in Egypt, for they had come at the invitation of a Khedive who was now dead, and could be forced to evacuate the country by the new Khedive, especially if he were sustained in his request by the rest of the European Powers. The Khedive financed Kamil to go to France, ostensibly to get a law degree, but really to carry out a press campaign to swing European public opinion against the British occupation of Egypt. The campaign did not move the Powers, nor did it move Cromer. Kamil then returned to Egypt to raise support for a nationalist movement that would force an evacuation of his country.

By then the British government had made over one hundred promises to evacuate Egypt but entrenched themselves even more securely. Cromer laboured to prove to the world that there was no Egyptian nation, for although Egypt had a population of nine million natives and less than one million aliens, who possessed a great deal of the wealth of the country, by his lights the Egyptians did not really count. Kamil, on the other hand, laboured to show that Egyptians did form a nation, one which demanded independence from foreign tutelage, and a constitutional government of Egyptians ruling for the benefit of Egyptians. Cromer paid little attention to the nationalist cause, for he thought it was made up of unimportant young men, whom he allowed to let off steam, believing the presence of the British army to be the ultimate guarantee of a continuing British presence in Egypt. He also found a number of Egyptians among the elite who were willing to collaborate with the British presence and to carry on the Veiled Protectorate.

The Egyptian nationalists soon became a thorn in Cromer's side and a vociferous element in Egyptian political life. Kamil had a devoted following among students, and they enthusiastically followed his directives in setting up strikes and demonstrations to protest against various unpopular measures. Strikes and massive demonstrations became a constant feature of Egyptian national life from that time to this day.

By the turn of the century Cromer had rendered Egypt solvent, albeit at the expense of Egyptian industry, and had transformed agriculture into a monoculture, cotton, to feed the mills of Lancashire. The cultivation of tobacco was prohibited and an excise tax imposed on imported tobacco helped to balance the budget. Attempts to set up local industries were discouraged by Cromer, who loaded them with tariffs equal to the taxes paid on imported goods, rendering them non-competitive. Textiles, which should have thrived using Egyptian cotton, were deliberately discouraged so that cotton could be exported. Egypt was relegated to becoming a provider of raw materials for Britain. For that reason agricultural and irrigation projects gained an overwhelming importance in government planning. In 1902 a dam was built at Aswan to store water and increase the acreage of arable land. The dam caused a problem of rising subsoil water, causing waterlogging of roots through lack of drainage and a problem of salination. Until an adequate drainage system was set up, crops were damaged and the Egyptian fallah suffered great hardship, as indeed did the landowner. Ironically enough, these are the same problems that face the new High Dam and plague Egyptian agriculture today.

Throughout the Cromer period a new phenomenon appeared – that of brigandage in the rural areas. The fallahin saw their traditional way of life replaced by a new, different one where nearly all crops were grown for export, thereby diminishing those grown for consumption; where new laws were passed which they neither understood nor even learned about; and where the new cash-crop economy demanded an outlay of capital which they did not have, causing them to fall into debt and lose their land. Those among them who had been so displaced took to brigandage and to acts of violence to protest against the encroachment of government on their lives – in Hobsbawmian terms they became 'primitive rebels'. The previous much vaunted security of the roads in Egypt was now replaced by violence and insecurity, a phenomenon Cromer and his administration failed to understand.

More unrest was to surface as the result of the events in Dinshwai in 1906. Dinshwai was a small village in the delta which had been used for pigeon shooting by some British officers, much to the dismay of the peasants who made a livelihood selling the birds they raised and bred. The following year the officers once again attacked the pigeons but this time the fallahin were ready for them; they attacked the officers, beat them with staves and disarmed them. One of the officers managed to escape and, in the heat of the August noonday sun, ran back to the camp for help. He died outside the camp of heat-stroke aggravated by concussion. The villagers were arrested and tried on charges of 'crimes of violence against the officers and men of the army of occupation'.

A special court martial was set up, which tried fifty-two accused in thirty minutes. Four men were sentenced to be hanged for the death by sunstroke of one British officer, while two men were sentenced to penal servitude for life; six men were given seven years' imprisonment and others were sentenced to various strokes of the lash. The entire village, men, women and children, were forced out of their huts to watch the executions and the floggings carried out. The severity of the sentences, which induced protests in the House of Commons in England, could only be explained by a loss of nerve. To the Egyptian nationalists that event was the last straw. It roused an emotion that was deep and long-lasting, an indictment of the occupation. Folk poets invented odes about Dinshwai, which were sung in all the villages, rousing feelings of animosity on the part of the fallah.

A Liberal government came to power in England and in 1907 Cromer, realizing he would no longer have the free hand in Egypt that he had had in the past, resigned. The nationalist movement was well-established and independent of the ruler by that time, and pushed for greater autonomy in administrative matters. A national assembly, one with more power, was elected and opposition to the occupation now found a channel for expressing its views openly and in a more organized fashion.

The war years brought a hiatus to political wrangling. Fearing the Khedive's pro-Ottoman proclivities, the British government deposed him while he was on a trip to the imperial capital, and appointed his uncle with the title of sultan to mark the distance between Egypt and Turkey when Turkey entered the war as an ally of Germany. With the agreement of the Egyptian government of the day, the British administration declared Egypt a British Protectorate, pronounced martial law, and promised that, once the war was over, the status of Egypt would be re-examined.

Throughout the war years the fallahin and those Egyptians who were on fixed salaries, such as government employees, suffered from inflation. Worse still, the fallahin were forced under corvée-like conditions (which had been abolished decades earlier) to go and dig ditches in Palestine for the British army. Beasts of burden were also commandeered for the army, leaving the fallahin with nothing to pull their ploughs or turn their waterwheels. Whatever friendly feelings the fallahin might have harboured for the British presence in Egypt, totally evaporated as the price of foodstuffs rose, and food, requisitioned for the army, became rare, threatening some areas with famine. War profiteering undoubtedly made things much worse, for while the British army protested that it paid good prices for all the things it took, the fallah saw little of that money and believed that he had gone back to the days of the three C's – the *curbaj* (lash), the corvée and corruption – the very things Cromer had proudly claimed to have destroyed.

During the war years Egyptian politicians speculated about the future of Egypt after the war. The various declarations made by the Allies during the war aroused hopes that independence might be in the offing, especially when President Wilson made public his Fourteen

Points. Self-determination became the keyword in everybody's mouth, and a group of politicians met to plan the future of Egypt as an imminently independent country, or at least one that would have a modicum of home-rule. That group of men constituted themselves into a delegation, in Arabic a *wafd*, and in November 1918 met with Sir Reginald Wingate, the British High Commissioner, to request they be allowed to proceed to the Paris Peace Conference and present Egypt's case. During that meeting one of the delegates told Wingate they were asking for complete independence, which became their goal. The British government in London refused the request of the wafd in no uncertain terms and agitation broke out in the country, encouraged by the nationalists and the government of the day and the sultan. By then the sultan was Prince Fuad, the youngest of the deposed Khedive Ismail's sons. Nationalist agitation sought to force a recognition of Egypt's right to plead her case in Paris and to choose her own representatives. Saad Zaghlul, a friend of Cromer's and a former cabinet minister (appointed by Cromer) as well as the elected vice-president of the national assembly, was chosen as the leader of the wafd.

Throughout 1919 Egypt was rife with agitation. Zaghlul was arrested and deported to Malta, which signalled an explosion of violence in all regions in support of the national leader. Some of the rural areas used the revolution as an excuse to break away from the central government and re-establish village unity by creating their own rural republic. For different reasons violence became endemic until finally the British government released the prisoners and allowed them to proceed to Paris.

Unfortunately for the Egyptians the British cabinet did not share their plans for the future of Egypt and the concessions offered the nationalists were turned down by the Egyptians, who once again took to the streets with violence. Zaghlul was once again deported and acts of terrorism continued until a new British High Commissioner, Lord Allenby, the hero of the western campaigns, forced the British government into making some concessions. In 1922 the

Protectorate over Egypt was abolished, martial law removed, and the country declared independent. That independence was hedged by a number of restrictions that rendered it well nigh void. However, a constituent council was given the task of preparing a constitution and the nationalists were freed from their exile. A liberal experiment was about to be tried in Egypt. That experiment was supposedly to grant Egypt a constitutional form of government, to institute representation and political parties, freedom of speech, the right to opposition – that is, all the trappings of a modern, democratic, representative government that operated in favour of the majority and not of a select elite. The reality turned out to be far distant from the dream, as we shall see in the next chapter, which is an account of attempts to institute liberal government on the part of some and attempts to oppose such a government on the part of others.

5 The liberal experiment, 1922–52

When the British government issued a unilateral declaration of Egyptian independence in 1922 they reserved four points of contention for future negotiations. These were: the defence of Egypt against foreign aggression or interference; the security of the communications of the British empire (that is the Suez Canal); the protection of foreign interests and of minorities; and the Sudan and its status.

A caretaker cabinet organized general elections, while the constituent committee, composed of the best legal brains, began preparing the ultimate constitution. Saad Zaghlul and his companions were released from exile in the Seychelles and returned to campaign for the elections. Their opponents, who had once been members of the Wafd – by now a political party – but had disagreed with Zaghlul's authoritarian style, formed a party of their own, the Liberal Constitutionalists (al-Ahrar al-Dusturiyyun).

The constituent committee was to meet with problems early on, as King Fuad, who was an autocrat, did not anticipate a constitution that would limit his authority or would even have strong powers of enforcement. The members of the constituent committee held the opposite view. The document that finally emerged was a compromise between the ideal and the real; it was a defective constitution, but the king refused to sign any other and was backed by the British government. The constitution vested legislative power in the king and a bicameral parliament. The king chose and appointed the prime minister and could dismiss the cabinet and postpone and prorogue parliament. He appointed the president of the senate and two-fifths of its members. The king was therefore given too much power, a power he used to undermine the workings of parliament ; not a single house ever fell through a vote of no confidence, but equally no house sat through its allotted period of time. Parliament was inevitably dismissed by the king, who preferred to rule through individuals who had no popular standing and represented no political party, rather than through the popularly elected parties. Rule was more often by decree than by parliamentary laws.

The only political party which had any grassroots backing was the Wafd Party, led by Zaghlul, who had tremendous charisma and could charm his audience into believing that they were Zaghlul, the epitome of the man in the street. While Zaghlul was really an arrogant man who despised almost all his colleagues, he came from a fallah background and so could talk in the idiom of the fallah and make the fallah identify with him, unlike the rest of the politicians, few of whom had that gift. The members of the Liberal Constitutionalist Party, for example, were men who identified with vested interests and did not believe the common touch was necessary. For that reason they never appealed to the masses and always remained a minority party that identified with the wealthy. The Wafd also was a party of wealthy landowners and the difference in political platforms between the two parties was insignificant, for they were really groupings around different personalities, each having a different campaigning style but both having the same goals.

Elections were held in January 1924 and their outcome was a foregone conclusion, a landslide for the Wafd which won 151 seats, leaving 7 for the Liberals. Zaghlul became prime minister, the first fallah Egyptian to occupy that position. By so doing he had displaced the old Turco-Circassian elite in favour of a new elite of native Egyptians, who from then on became the main ruling element in the country. Zaghlul – who was dubbed 'the king of hearts', as opposed to the real king sitting in the palace at Abdin, and the uncrowned king, the British High Commissioner, sitting in his palace at Qasr al-Doubara – had to toe a fine line in that tripartite power setting. Behind Zaghlul lay the power of the majority, manifest in the mob which followed Zaghlul whenever he called upon it and shouted slogans in his favour all the way to the palace to prove to the king that Zaghlul was their spokesman, not some Turkish king who barely spoke Arabic. When Fuad first came to Egypt, having been brought up abroad with his exiled father the Khedive Ismail, he spoke little if any Arabic; when he did learn Arabic he always spoke it with a foreign accent and used foreign expressions translated into Arabic, which consequently sounded strange.

The personal antagonism that existed between Fuad and Zaghlul affected their relationship, which was always tense. But were we to leave the personal element out of their relationship we find the two men were each struggling to impose a principle of government. Fuad sought to sidestep the constitution and rule as an autocrat whenever he could; he therefore believed he need not consult his premier nor even parliament, which he termed a flock of sheep fit only to be led. Zaghlul was fighting real constitutional battles and had to resort to threats of resignation, or worse, to get the king to rule according to the terms of the constitution. He used the power of the mob to threaten the king with outbreaks of violence if the king did not abide by his legal interpretations, and on several occasions the king was forced to accede to his premier.

Zaghlul believed that his most important mission was to negotiate an Anglo-Egyptian treaty that would settle the four reserved points and free Egypt from continued British interference in its political life. He failed to negotiate such a treaty and before further events could unfold a tragedy struck.

Throughout the years following the 1919 revolution the country had been seething with violence and unrest. Acts of terrorism had been carried out by a number of secret organizations, all believing they were helping the nationalist cause. One of these organizations had been created as a paramilitary arm of the Wafd. None of the members of the Wafd, save Zaghlul and the members of the paramilitary group, knew about the existence of that apparatus. The leader of the group, who had unsuccessfully stood for a seat in parliament and held a grudge against Zaghlul for not helping him obtain his seat, organized the murder of the commander-in-chief of the Egyptian army (the Sirdar), an Englishman named Sir Lee Stack. The death of Stack, a close friend of Allenby, the High Commissioner, was blamed by Allenby on Zaghlul and his fiery speeches, which Allenby believed incited violence, and he determined to teach Zaghlul a lesson. He presented the Egyptian government with an ultimatum which demanded the withdrawal of all Egyptian army units stationed in the Sudan (a punitive clause that had nothing to do with the assassination), as well as an indemnity of half a million pounds.

Shocked at the assassination, which he believed had ruined his career, Zaghlul signed the indemnity cheque, refused the other clauses, deemed insulting, and resigned. His career was effectively ruined for he was never again allowed to become premier by the British government even though he was head of the majority party. Parliament was dissolved by the king after having sat for a total of nine months.

The British government disapproved of their representative's actions and soon recalled him, replacing him by Sir George Lloyd, who determined to out-Cromer Cromer in Egypt and to make the Egyptians toe the line. What Cromer could do two decades earlier was no longer possible in a country which was theoretically independent with a constitution and a parliament of its own. Soon he and various cabinets were to come into conflict. Lloyd, a narrow-minded right-wing Tory imperialist, was a firm believer in gunboat diplomacy and called out the gunboats at the slightest provocation. He considered Egyptians irrational and emotional and used to say that the hot winds of spring (the *khamasin*) unsettled their minds, so when he saw the jacaranda trees in bloom he knew it was time to call out the gunboats. Lloyd kept Zaghlul away from power, and in this he may have been mistaken, for Zaghlul was perhaps the only man who could have negotiated a treaty with Britain and made it palatable to his people, for he dominated the political life of the country as no other politician would do until the fifties. When he was elected president of the lower house Zaghlul kept the members in line by a fiercely barked *uskut* (silence), when anyone grew too longwinded, and the members accepted it from him whereas, coming from anyone else, it would have been shouted down.

Zaghlul died in 1927 at the age of seventy. He had been venerated by his countrymen and respected by both king and opposition. His influence on political life, though strong, was not always for the better. He had introduced a system of patronage into political life, and a system of violence and of public demonstrations as a weapon against the opposition. Through his autocracy he had alienated the most brilliant brains, and had set up a personal form of rule. He had sown many of the public ills that have beset political life to the present day. During his lifetime he had dominated the political scene by virtue of his political acumen and the force of his personality, but the system he set up was flawed, and in the hands of lesser men – like his successor Mustafa al-Nahhas – the flaws were clearly revealed. He had served his country by his devotion to parliamentary procedures and to the constitution, and by his battles for a democratic form of government, when the king wished to impose an autocracy more fitted to the past century. Since he had to give battle to both king and British representative, the cards were stacked against him but he struggled against them to the end of his days.

Subsequent attempts at negotiating a treaty with Britain met with little success. In 1926 before Zaghlul's death a Wafd–Liberal coalition had come close to guiding a treaty through, but Zaghlul died before the treaty was ratified and Zaghlul's successors, who wanted the glory of negotiating a treaty to be theirs, destroyed it. A dog-in-the-manger attitude became characteristic of political infighting, where personal animosities and jealousies became more important than principles and the country's common interest. The king was always ready to dangle the lure of the premiership to any politician, while the leader of the Wafd, Nahhas, was an inept parliamentarian who allowed parliament to degenerate into an instrument of party obstruction, had little control over his followers and was too easily swayed by his companions.

The three-sided political manoeuvres that necessitated a coalition of two against the third marred political life and injected an element of intrigue into it. Sooner or later either the king or the political party in power had to go to the British High Commissioner as the final arbiter, instead of appealing to parliament. The liberal experiment was so loaded as to be doomed almost from the start.

In 1929 the king managed to bring down a Wafd government when Nahhas was accused of improper behaviour in a legal case he had defended. He was innocent of the charge, but the king used it as an excuse to bring down the government and appoint a Liberal cabinet, which promptly requested parliament be suspended for a period of three years. Fuad seemed to be correct when he described constitutional life as a farce, when those who were supposed to uphold the constitution, the Liberal Constitutionalists, were the ones who requested its suspension when they found themselves in the position of a minority in parliament. The new government was unpopular for its rule of the 'iron fist', and for its aloofness from the common man. Its paternalistic attitude grated on the public and alienated them. The new cabinet came at the same time as an economic crisis swept the rest of the world, ushering in years of depression that lasted in Egypt until 1933 and caused the fallahin, who formed 82 per cent of the population, to suffer acute hardship.

Egypt had been turned into a monoculture by Cromer, and from 1923 to 1926 it had enjoyed a boom in cotton production which accentuated the subsequent depression even more. Parliament was dominated by landowners who did little for the small farmer or even for the industrial labourer, small though his numbers were. Half the land was owned by 22,016 large landowners, that is, half the land was controlled by 2 per cent of the population, while 61 per cent of the population controlled 300,000 faddans. When Fuad had come to the throne his land holdings had been fairly modest, a mere 800 faddans. By the time his son Faruq was forced to abdicate in 1952 the royal estates had grown by various means to cover 100,000 faddans. The rich landowners had cooperated in turning Egypt into a monoculture, for it had made them wealthy, but it was also to tie them closely to Britain, the major buyer of cotton, and one which the landowners could ill afford to alienate on pain of bankruptcy. That economic link with Britain was naturally reflected in the political relationship between the two countries and explained the reluctance of Egyptian politicians to push the British government too hard.

The perception of a rich landowner is different from that of a village *umda* (chief), and quite different from that of the landless fallah or the sharecropper. Parliament refused to permit the creation of fallah labour unions, or even of trade unions; it was only nearly two decades later that a minimum wage for agricultural workers was enacted. Wages of rural workers depended on the law of supply and demand and by 1929 these wages had fallen to pre-1920 prices, only to fall to pre-World War I prices by 1933. Money wages had fallen 50 per cent at a time when the price of food and clothing had risen considerably. The man in the street blamed the depression on the Liberal Constitutionalists and coined the slogan. 'Better the fire of the Wafd than the paradise of the Liberals'. Demonstrations broke out against the government and were brutally repressed. In one incident passers-by as well as demonstrators were assaulted by the police. This incident allowed the king to show his displeasure with the cabinet and resort to blackmail, with an implied threat of dismissal, in order to force the cabinet to do his bidding, for after all, he, and not the will of the people, had brought the cabinet to power.

In the midst of local turmoil the premier decided to try his hand at negotiating an Anglo-Egyptian treaty, but the British government was conscious that no treaty negotiated by a cabinet without parliamentary approval would be worthwhile, so the premier returned to Egypt and resigned. A caretaker cabinet organized elections which brought the Wafd once more to power, for whenever free elections were organized the Wafd won with a large majority. Yet that cabinet lasted a mere six months until the premier, Nahhas, resigned in a fit of pique, assuming that a public outcry would force the king to bring him back to power. Nahhas was no Zaghlul and the king was only too glad to be rid of him and to install a cabinet under Ismail Pasha Sidqi that was to usher in the most repressive period of government Egypt had known. Sidqi suspended parliament once more, amended the constitution to diminish suffrage and so weaken support for the Wafd, and ruled with a rod of iron. His government was to become a byword for corruption and the abuse of power.

A new British High Commissioner, Sir Percy Loraine, had been appointed to replace Lord Lloyd (the former Sir George Lloyd), and he was content to let Sidqi rule as he pleased and would not lift a finger to help the opposition oust the cabinet. All he did was to advise the opposition to unite its ranks. Daily demonstrations filled the streets with cries of 'Down with the king', and an attempt was made to assassinate Sidqi. The Wafd was forbidden to tour the country or to speak in public, but they frequently infringed the law and tried to rouse the population to oppose the government even more. Newspapers were censored. Adversity finally brought the political parties together, but there was little they could do to oust the cabinet so long as the king and the High Commissioner sustained it.

The Egyptians believed there were three determinants of British policy in Egypt. The first was the British would always support the king since they had brought him to power and would never allow him to be ousted by a popular movement. The second was whatever steps British officials took in Egypt they were taken with British, not Egyptian, interests in mind. Lastly, a cabinet would stay in power only so long as it was supported by the British, for the minute that support was withdrawn the cabinet fell. Thus Egyptians firmly believed Sidqi's cabinet was supported by the British government. The younger Egyptians, especially the students, who had been made an active part of political life under Zaghlul, who had used them in demonstrations, became disillusioned by their political leadership. They had assumed that a constitution and a parliament would be preliminaries to the establishment of a truly democratic system, and would rapidly be followed by an Anglo-Egyptian treaty that would settle matters with Britain and bring to an end both interference in internal matters and the British military presence in Egypt. These things had not happened and loss of hope became a characteristic of the thirties. Disillusion with politicians, allied to a recession that affected everyone, even rich landowners, caused a number of movements and associations to rise and challenge the hegemony of the Wafd over the masses. Foremost among these associations was the Society of Muslim Brethren founded by an obscure elementary school teacher named Sheikh Hasan al-Banna.

It would seem that when an acute economic depression allied to feelings of political disillusion overwhelms the population, it turns inwards to its own roots for answers to its dilemma. In this case it was a return to Islamic themes, to the consolation offered by religion, to the assurance that its culture would not become overwhelmed by a foreign import but would survive and overcome alien ideologies. Hasan al-Banna preached a fundamentalist religious revival and his message soon spread beyond the town of Ismailiyya where he first started to preach. By 1930, when he moved to Cairo, the movement had gathered momentum until it grew to rival the Wafd in its grassroots support, more specifically in urban areas. Al-Banna brought an alternative to the eternal bickering of political parties over power. He told people to help one another, to strive for a better world, to turn to their religion and seek their answers there rather than from the political parties. The newly urbanized masses, driven from the rural areas by the recession to seek jobs in the city, found little comfort there. The old traditional associations that in the past had cocooned the urban workers in the warmth of a guild, or a Sufi fraternity, had disappeared with the process of modernization, leaving little to take their place. There were no trade unions or labour associations of any kind. There was precious little in the way of public assistance or of social welfare; new immigrants were helpless and easily exploited by those who hired them. The Muslim Brethren offered an alternative; they offered associations which embraced all members of the family; schools which taught traditional Muslim learning instead of the newfangled secular education taught in government schools; self-help where jobs were found for those who needed them. There was also an association for women which taught them religion and tried to help them overcome their alienation from a new and unfamiliar milieu. The members of the association were always cleanly and neatly dressed in modest attire, for each one of them felt that he was a living example of his faith. Members of the association found themselves engulfed in a movement, indoctrinated and subject to the dictates of the Supreme Guide, Hasan al-Banna. There was no room for dissent. All the frustrations of a society that was undergoing change and was in the throes of a recession were blamed on the influence of the Europeans, who had introduced foreign elements into Egypt and alienated Egyptians from their traditional ways of life in order to dominate and exploit them. The rejection of the British presence, the essence of the national movement, was equated with a rejection of everything foreign, which was believed to be encouraged by the British.

Soon the Brethren became a political power to contend with, for their following rapidly grew and included not only the urban poor, who formed the bulk of the membership, but also the middle classes, who were equally disenchanted with their government and its economic policies and its inability to do much to oust the British from the land.

Other groupings were also spawned by that period of depression and political chaos. Fascist movements in imitation of Mussolini's organization soon appeared, among which was Misr al-Fatat (Young Egypt), which put its small group of followers into green shirts. This called forth a reaction on the part of the Wafd, who set up a youth organization of bully boys and dressed them in blue shirts. A small communist party tried to organize workers and did have limited success among them. None of these groupings had the popular appeal of the Muslim Brethren, who talked in an idiom the people understood, who reassured the masses that religion would find a way out for them, and who actively sought to organize and to help their members find jobs and set up businesses.

Sidqi, who was a financial wizard, did little for the economy, probably because his inclinations were to favour the moneyed classes and his talents were not directed towards helping the mass of the people, in whom he had little interest. The annual per capita income fell to £8 for the years 1930 to 1933, where it had been £12 in 1913. The consumption of cereals and pulses had declined by almost half a million tons for a population that had increased by three million people. In 1930 Sidqi had even placed a prohibitive tariff on the import of wheat, when the acreage of land planted with wheat had diminished as a result of increasing cotton demand. The members of the urban working classes were thus paying a subsidy to the agricultural population of £5 million per year. The thirties were years of unrest and violence, and in the forties famine riots were to crown the years of want and hardship.

Sidqi assumed that British acquiescence in his form of repression was a sign of approval of his government and, motivated by the same ego that moved his colleagues, he too sought an Anglo-Egyptian accord that would single him out for the praise of history and the adulation of future generations. Before the negotiations could take place, his government fell. Rumours of peculation and profiteering on the part of Sidqi and the members of his family had been spreading. A public scandal exploded over rumours the government had used torture in a legal case. The case had appeared before the Cour de Cassation and the president of the court had demanded a public investigation. Tension had been growing between Sidqi and the king, for the king had begun to look upon Sidqi as expendable and came to believe he could appoint his own puppets to the premiership without bothering to make his premier at least half-way credible. All these factors together brought Sidqi to resign and the Wafd to power.

The Sidqi regime, the longest period of rule by decree since 1922, had set a pattern for government coercion which was countered by violence on the part of the opposition and the people. Violence became entrenched as part of political life. A greater element of unscrupulousness entered political life and any means were justified for the end of seizing and retaining control of government. Having spent years outside power, the Wafd was determined never to let go of power again. Enmity between the monarch and his people was established, for the people well knew who had brought Sidqi to power and maintained him there. The gap between the rulers and the ruled widened. While the ruling classes came to see government as a prize for which the various parties struggled among themselves, the people came to see the parties as representing nothing more than vested interests and their own social class.

Though many Egyptian politicians were nationalists genuinely trying to achieve independence for their country, at the same time they were landowners who refused to consider the welfare of their fallahin alongside their own. Dependent as they were on the British cotton market, they feared bankruptcy if they did not follow British orders; as a result the nationalist movement had few teeth to it. Sooner or later the police, led by British officers, would dominate the situation, a pliable premier would be found, and business would go on as usual. Some Egyptians finally came to the realization that true political independence could only come with economic independence. Landowners could not succeed in negotiating a treaty that granted Egypt anything more than nominal independence, but, once the country was industrialized, its economic links with the occupying power would weaken, even disappear, and real independence might be effected.

Industrialization received its impetus with the founding of Bank Misr and its affiliates by Talaat Harb and his associates. Many of the investors in the new bank were landowners, since they were the only natives with capital to spare. A tariff reform in 1930 allowed native industries protection and a fighting chance of succeeding against foreign competition. The occupation had helped foreign firms establish themselves in Egypt, while the terms of the capitulations gave them an extra advantage in that they were not subject to local laws or taxes. Thus, until the tariff reforms, local industries were doomed to failure.

The new industrial elite offered little political challenge to the landowning bourgeoisie because they usually came from the same milieu. The landowners financed industry and the new industrialists – some of whom were professionals – sought to acquire land as a means of establishing their social credentials. This merely served to drive up the price of land and to create more landless fallahin. In brief, the landowning class and the new industrial bourgeoisie fused and intermarried until they became indistinguishable. That fusion explains why parliament passed as few labour laws for industrial workers as it did for rural workers. Although the principle of a native-owned industry was sound as it led in the direction of economic independence, both native and foreign industries exploited the worker and did little to improve his conditions. Locally owned industries were still no match for foreign industries, which owned as much as two-thirds of the country's total industrial wealth.

A few labour organizations came into existence, sometimes sponsored by one of the political parties, or even by a maverick member of the royal family, Abbas Halim, who found the best means of annoying his cousin the king was to head a trade union and pose as a leader of the working poor. The Wafd tried to organize a labour union, but basically unions were organized and led by middle-class professionals, not by workers, so their effectiveness was at best questionable. In 1932 H. B. Butler from the International Federation of Trade Unions was invited to come on a fact-finding mission because of labour unrest. His recommendations were not implemented until over a decade later, after famine riots had broken out. In 1933 a child-labour law was passed, which stopped some of the worst industrial horrors, and another law limited working hours for women to a maximum of nine hours a day. In 1936 a bill made the employer liable for any on-the-job accident. A labour office was established, but it was set up in the police station to discourage any complaints. Anyone coming to the labour office with a grievance knew his name would be taken down by the police and he would be marked a troublemaker.

All social problems in Egypt had been shelved by successive governments with the excuse that they had more important matters to worry about, notably negotiating a treaty with England. Until that treaty was negotiated no one confronted Egypt's problems of disease, ignorance, and poverty. By 1936 a new problem was added – that of overpopulation. Many refused to believe that overpopulation was a problem for it supplied extra labour for the cotton crop, which is labour-intensive. But since the increase in population had not been met by an increase in agricultural land or in massive industrialization the problem was to become more acute with the passage of time.

The complacency of successive governments and their total lack of social awareness allowed the political system to continue undisturbed by local events. Whenever violence and unrest surfaced it was met by police repression and a sop or two in the form of labour legislation, which was often not implemented. As for the rural areas, these were far apart and even more disorganized than the urban areas, and at the mercy of the landowners who dominated the land and parliament. The intellectuals were aware of these problems in the country and, though they spoke out against them, few listened among the high and the mighty; they were busy fighting for power or trying to negotiate a treaty. Meanwhile the undercurrent of dissatisfaction on the part of the working poor, students and unemployed intellectuals was growing.

Egyptian intellectuals had accused the British occupation of two major ills: keeping the country uneducated to justify a continued occupation and killing off Egyptian industry in favour of lop-sided agricultural development. Both education and industrialization were to develop in the thirties. Equally important was the emancipation of women, which became a plank in the nationalist platform and occurred earlier in Egypt than in any other Arab or Muslim country. When the nationalists were arrested during the events of 1919, their women took up the movement and demonstrated, veiled, in the streets. Working-class women were not veiled, for segregation was a luxury that only the affluent, and those who sought to imitate them, could afford. It was only right that the women of the elite be the ones to give a lead in shedding the veil. There are two stories about how this came about. One story claims that Hoda Shaarawi, wife of one of the early Wafd founders, and daughter of the largest landowner in Egypt, was returning from a trip to Europe in 1923, where she had represented Egypt in a feminist convention, and as her ship approached the harbour at Alexandria, threw her veil overboard and landed unveiled. Her gesture was imitated by the other women and from then on women of the elite went unveiled, a step that was rapidly imitated by all other women.

The other version is that the elite women decided to give a tea for some charity affair, at which they would present *tableaux vivants*. As was customary, women sat on one side of the hall, men on the other, with a screen between the two to shield the women from the eyes of the men. At a certain signal the screen came down and the men saw the women unveiled. One uncharitable wit claimed that when this happened someone shouted, 'For Heaven's sake, veil them up again.' Once the women were unveiled, they took part in the public life of the country, not by seeking to obtain positions and earn a living, which they did not need to do, but simply by taking over all the social services of the country. They set up charitable foundations which organized hospitals, dispensaries and clinics all over the land. They established orphanages, schools for girls, and institutions to teach working-class girls a trade. Where their husbands spent their time in political squabbles, these women set a better example by managing to work together in an admirable fashion. It is thanks to them that Egypt has the social services that exist today. The women were so efficient that in 1948 the army asked them to organize a nursing corps, and later on asked them to set up rehabilitation centres. Their efforts resulted in supplying the country with two million hospital beds where people of any class could be treated – free of charge for the poor and with a fee for those who could afford it. Every major town and village ended by acquiring a dispensary or a clinic, thanks to the efforts of the women, who did it all through contributions. They bullied, cajoled, even blackmailed the rich into donating land and money to set up their institutions, and in times of epidemics they toured the devastated areas, brought medicines and food to the needy and cajoled the sick into agreeing to go to the hospitals where they could get proper medical care.

Education also progressed, although not as rapidly as desired. Under Cromer the budget for education was about 1 per cent, a demonstration of his lack of interest in public education. In 1910 the budget for education went up to 3.4 per cent and by 1930–1 it had reached almost 11 per cent of a much larger total expenditure. In 1925 a law was passed making elementary education compulsory in an effort to eradicate illiteracy. This meant the erection of school buildings and the training of teachers on a large scale, but as funds were not available the law remained a dead letter. However, the rate of illiteracy began to drop slightly, although most of the real gains were made under Nasser so that today 70–80 per cent of children of school age are enrolled in primary schools.

On the other hand, secondary school education was regarded as a preparation towards a career or a profession. It was the means which led to the prestigious world of the professional, or better still, the bureaucracy, which offered security of tenure, a pension plan and a chance of reaching the upper echelons of government. Secondary school and university students represented an elite and their importance in society as yet far outweighed their contributions to that society. They were participants in political agitation on a grand scale, first against the British occupation, then against the monarch and the government. The years 1935–6 were named the 'years of youth' because they were years of student riots. They were also years of disenchantment with political leaders and of fear for the students' professional future. For while the population had grown, the capacity of the country to absorb them had not and by 1937 Egypt suffered the problem of unemployment among intellectuals in a country that was largely illiterate. 7,500 baccalaureate holders and 3,500 university graduates were jobless. Those who graduated from foreign schools and spoke foreign languages found jobs in foreign firms, but since members of minorities were the ones who frequented foreign schools, that simply added to the bitterness of the native Egyptians.

In the forties free university education was instituted, which helped overstrain every classroom and lecture hall and diminished the quality of education. The problem was to worsen after the revolution of 1952, when universities multiplied rapidly but the number of professors did not. The presence of a large mass of educated and unemployed people destabilized society and created a mass of discontented and alienated intellectuals.

Under the impetus of the recent Italian occupation of Ethiopia, its presence in Cyrenaica, and a growing fear of a second world war, all the political parties came together in a coalition to negotiate an Anglo-Egyptian treaty. Before the treaty could be negotiated King Fuad died in April 1936, leaving behind his son Faruq, still a minor, who succeeded to the throne the following year. Fuad had reigned as both sultan and king for nineteen years, having died at the age of sixty-eight. A despot at heart, he had done his best to undermine constitutional life, a principle of government in which he did not believe. He was ruthless and vindictive, though he had a keen intelligence and a thorough knowledge of all that went on in the country, including knowing the least scandal about any member of the elite. He worked hard at his job and, while his government disliked him, they respected his grasp of problems and his knowledge of internal affairs. His son was never anything more than a playboy masquerading as a king. Both father and son had in common the ability to amass riches. Fuad had founded several institutions of learning, such as the Royal Geographic Society and, more importantly, had been instrumental in inducing his sister to donate funds and jewellery to erect the buildings of what became the Fuad I University, now known as the University of Cairo The first rector of that institution was Ahmad Lutfi al-Sayyid, a leading intellectual in the country, and one of Fuad's *bêtes noires*.

National elections once again brought a Wafd majority to power with Nahhas as premier, but the parties came together in 1936 as a United Front to send a delegation to England to negotiate the Anglo-Egyptian Treaty. Earlier attempts at treaties had failed for a variety of reasons, but by then Egyptian politicians were willing to make con-cessions they had turned down earlier, because they feared a world war. The outcome was a treaty that gave Egypt little more than the terms it had been offered a decade earlier, but which was hailed by most parties as a successful outcome to an impasse.

Individual politicians objected to some of the clauses of the treaty. For example, some feared the implications of a treaty which required the Egyptian government to render Britain assistance in the event of war or 'an apprehended international emergency'. Some objected to the stipulation that the Egyptian government undertake to build roads to facilitate British troop movements within the country in the case of an emergency. By and large most of the politi-cians felt the treaty offered Egypt substantial gains. It ended the occu-pation in a legal sense, although not in a physical one, for British troops were still to be stationed in the Canal Zone. It gave Egypt British support to get the country admitted into the League of Nations as an independent country; it placed the responsibility for protection of foreigners and minorities with the Egyptian authorities – the only one of the Four Reserved Points to be settled. It promised to assist Egypt in abolishing the capitulations (see p. 84) which continued to plague any government and which finally came to an end in 1948.

The treaty was to last for twenty years, when it would be reopened for negotiation, and if no agreement was reached between both parties it would be submitted to the Council of the League of Nations. Ambassadors were exchanged, but the British Ambassador in Egypt was always to occupy the position of senior ambassador. While the terms of the treaty mentioned a joint protection of the Suez Canal by British and Egyptian forces, no Egyptian forces or civilians were allowed to enter the Canal Zone without the permission of British forces, and no Egyptian planes were allowed to fly over the Canal Zone. The Egyptian army was to be trained and armed by British officers and weapons, and all British officials employed in the Egyptian government were eventually to be phased out and replaced by Egyptian officials.

The terms of the treaty were described by Nahhas, who had led the delegation, in the usual hyperbole as terms of 'honour and independence'. Many thought quite differently and pointed out with justice that these same terms had been offered in the past and turned down by the Wafd as insufficient, because the Wafd had not then been party to the negotiations. In parliament the treaty was discussed before ratification and both Sidqi and Muhammad Mahmud, the leaders of the Liberal Constitutional Party, who had been members of the delegation, pointed out that the terms of the treaty did not give Egypt complete independence, but they also pointed to the fact that the Egyptian army was in no condition to undertake the defence of Egypt for some time to come and the country would therefore have to rely on British protection.

The general feeling was one of limited satisfaction that the treaty at least had changed the previous deadlock and would open the door to future negotiations, once fear of a world war had evaporated. The British army presence was to be unobtrusive, for troops would be relegated to the Canal Zone, instead of being stationed in the capital city, but they were still very much there, as events in 1942 and 1951 were to demonstrate. The section of the community which was the most dissatisfied with the treaty was that of the foreign residents. Many of them were of Greek, Levantine, Armenian and Italian origin and had long been established in Egypt and knew no other homeland, but preferred to keep their alien status and benefit from the capitulations. The occupation had allowed them preferential rights and the capitulations permitted them to make money but pay little in the way of taxes. Now they were threatened with being treated on a par with nationals. They would have to use native courts in cases of litigation and not rely on the mixed courts, where a majority of the judges were aliens, or on the consular courts in criminal cases. Some opted for Egyptian nationality, some opted to leave, while others opted to remain aliens and to stay, but at the same time transferring large amounts of money out of Egypt.

There were some slight financial gains for some Egyptians through the treaty, for while the population generally had to shoulder the heavy burden of building roads and barracks for the British army, the Egyptian government was allowed to appoint two members to the board of directors of the Suez Canal Company. The company raised its annual payment to Egypt by £300,000 and agreed to hire 35 per cent of its workforce from among the Egyptian population.

As a byproduct of the treaty of alliance, the military academy opened its doors wider to take in the sons of the middle and lower bourgeoisie, for the army needed an officer corps. 10 per cent of the students were allowed into the academy free of charge. The most famous officer to come from that poorer milieu was Gamal Abd al-Nasir, or Nasser as he came to be known in the West.

Once the treaty was negotiated, the Egyptian government could no longer use it as an excuse to shelve internal problems and was forced to face these with little knowledge of their ramifications or of their solutions. Institutions were weak at best and the personal element tended to rule the institutional. Intermediaries and patrons were appealed to and acted on behalf of their clients, so the institution was sidestepped in favour of the use, or abuse, of influence. And yet people in government positions had a high degree of moral rectitude and tried to act according to a notion of justice and fair play; those who were accused of corruption were well-known figures despised by the rest of the bureaucracy. Bribery was rare, although a handful of powerful individuals were notorious for accepting bribes. The government had no clear plan of how to reform problems that faced them and soon got bogged down in party infighting that conveniently put off any major overhaul of the administration.

King Faruq reached his majority in July 1937 and continued to perpetuate the conflict between palace and Wafd that his father had begun. The Wafd had been weakened by the defection of some of its abler members, who founded a new party named after Saad Zaghlul, the Saadist Party, to show that the Wafd had departed from the principles laid down by the founder of the party. There were in fact precious few principles and once again, whether Wafd or Saadist, they were groupings round individuals and differed in style and manner rather than in content or platform. Faruq was idolized by the population, who saw a young, handsome boy, who seemed to epitomize hope for the future and a new departure in government. He had a winning personality which attracted people, but also caused his mentors to spoil him and cater to his every whim. Conflict between him and the Wafd, and between him and the British Ambassador – the former High Commissioner – soon broke out, and Faruq too was threatened with deposition if he did not behave himself. The members of the royal entourage, who had been chosen by Fuad because they were inimical to the Wafd, encouraged Faruq to take a stand against the majority party, to come closer to the men of religion in al-Azhar, which was then led by a most enlightened rector, Sheikh al-Maraghi, and attempt to use al-Azhar as a lever against the Wafd.

When the Second World War broke out, Egypt was faced with an invasion from the western desert, where the Italian armies under Graziani were eventually defeated by Wavell, who drove the Italians out of Cyrenaica in March 1941. By the following month the British army was pushed back by Rommel's advance and it looked as though Egypt would soon be occupied by the Germans for by July 1942 German forces were within seventy miles of Alexandria. For that year, until November when the battle of Alamein finally forced Rommel's retreat from Egypt, it was touch and go. The British embassy burned its files, in preparation for an evacuation, and the Royal Air Force airport in Heliopolis was bombed every night. Food became scarce. Prices rose and some people took to hoarding. Ration cards were printed but they were ineffective. The poor suffered hunger and rioted, blaming the British army for their misery, and accusing them of eating the country's food.

Dissatisfaction with the terms of the treaty surfaced. It had become obvious that Egypt would have to spend a good deal of money and effort to provide facilities and amenities for the British army, which was rapidly growing in numbers as a consequence of the war. Furthermore, facilities for rest and recreation were also being provided by an entrepreneurial class which made money from war profiteering, military contracts, nightclubs and bars. The sight of so many uniformed soldiers walking about the streets of the main cities in search of amusement shocked the sensibilities of a population that was largely traditional, deeply religious, and which frowned on the bars and houses of prostitution that mushroomed. This feeling was especially high among the members of the Society for Muslim Brethren, who were outraged that their poorer women were opting for a life of sin through the lure of British gold. Their activities multiplied as they showed their followers that Muslim principles and ethics were infringed by the British presence. Few among the population cared about the issues for which a world war was being fought, or were even familiar with them. Hitler and Mussolini were names that meant little to them; many even believed the presence of the Germans might be used as a lever with which to drive out the British from Egypt once and for all. Even the king seemed to share that feeling and it was rumoured he was secretly plotting to hand over the country to the Axis powers. One of his mentors, General Aziz Ali al-Masri, who had been trained in the German military academy, made no bones about his sympathies for them.

Rommel's campaign and the people's adulation of him together with the king's contacts with the Axis powers, real or suspected, were twin disasters facing the British government, who decided to take drastic action. On 4 February 1942 the palace at Abdin was suddenly surrounded by British tanks and the king was offered an ultimatum: either Nahhas be appointed premier or the king would be deposed forthwith. Nahhas had obviously come to some prior agreement with the British ambassador over the government of the country during the war years and knew the king would be threatened if he did not accept a Wafd Party leadership. The party which had come into being on the strength of its opposition to the British presence in Egypt was now to collaborate with that very presence against the king. Some believed the Wafd was justified in agreeing to come to power in that fashion, on the strength of British tanks, but others despised the Wafd for accepting government in those circumstances. The king was forced to accede to British demands; Nahhas and the Wafd came to power and lasted until 1944, when the threat of Rommel had evaporated and the tide of war had turned in favour of the Allies.

The Wafd's acquiescence in British high-handedness shocked the population, which knew little of the issues involved and still regarded the king as its hero; from then on they began to look upon the Wafd as a less than nationalist party. Alternatives were sought to the party that was attracting to itself charges of nepotism, corruption and abuse of power that were made public by one of Nahhas's closest associates, Makram Ubaid, in a Black Book that rocked the country with its sensational revelations. Ubaid, Nahhas's *éminence grise* for a long time, had parted ways with his friend and, being a genuine nationalist who had never made money at the expense of his country or profited from any financial government deal, spelled out the extent of peculation, corruption and abuse of power. The Wafd government continued to stay in power, because the British authorities so willed, and no charges were ever brought against it.

The end of the war brought Egypt to join the United Nations and once more the question of negotiating the evacuation of British forces from Egypt surfaced. A new premier decided to take the case to the United Nations Security Council, according to the terms of the Anglo-Egyptian Treaty. The Council called upon Britain and Egypt to reopen negotiations, which was a lame decision, since the two sides could not agree. The treaty had stationed British forces in Egypt for twenty years, but the British government, occupied with other imperial problems, saw no need to change the situation or to modify any part of the treaty. The most urgent clause in the treaty was the one dealing with the Sudan. That territory, though supposedly under an Anglo-Egyptian condominium rule, was entirely administered by British officials, while the Egyptian share in government had been limited to footing the bill – until 1924, that is, when it ceased to do so. The Egyptians were now calling for the union of Egypt and the Sudan. Demonstrations appeared in the streets shouting such slogans as 'Egypt and the Sudan united' to which some wits had added another slogan, 'Egypt and the Sudan for us, and the British Isles if there's no fuss'. Many Sudanese did not want a union with Egypt; they preferred to acquire their own independence from both Egypt and Britain.

The hubbub over the treaty negotiations was to be replaced by a greater preoccupation with events in Palestine. Since 1936 when the first Arab general strike had broken out, many Egyptians had been worried about events in Palestine and the increasing Jewish presence there. Nahhas and his government had made a lot of sympathetic noises aimed at their Arab brethren in Palestine and in the other Arab countries, but they were secretly ordered by the British government to take no steps to raise either money or sympathy for the cause of the Palestinians. They were even ordered to prevent Palestinian leaders from speaking publicly in Egypt. The British government used the carrot and the stick on the Wafd and induced them to believe they would be endangering their chances for a revision of the treaty once the war was over if they interfered in affairs in Palestine.

During the war years nothing could be done to assist the Palestinians, who also waited out the war while the Zionists joined the Allies and in consequence received military training, which stood them in good stead when they embarked on their campaign against the Arabs, designed to oust them from certain areas and cities.

When Britain ended its mandate over Palestine in May 1948, war on the new state of Israel was declared by all the Arab countries, including Egypt. The Egyptian army was totally unprepared for war, for the army had no weapons save for the antiquated ones supplied by the British army, and almost no planes. Both the prime minister and the minister for defence had told the king that the country was not capable of going to war, and he had assured them that in that case he would refrain from a declaration of war. The next morning both men read in the morning newspapers that Egypt had declared war on Israel.

The course of the war was little short of disastrous. The king sent some of his closest companions to negotiate arms deals in Belgium. As a result they became millionaires, and it was even speculated that the king had also made a profit from these deals. But the artillery they had obtained exploded more frequently in the face of the Egyptian army than at the enemy, for most of the arms were defective World War II surplus. The Egyptian army captured the area of Gaza, but some of the army was besieged by the Israelis during the battle of al-Faluja. During that siege a young army officer often chatted across the lines with his Israeli counterparts and asked them how they had managed to get rid of the British presence in Palestine. That young officer was Gamal Abd al-Nasir (Nasser), later to become the leader of the revolution of 1952.

Eventually the war in Palestine provided a training ground not only for Egyptian officers and men but also for the paramilitary organizations of the Muslim Brethren who fought as volunteers in the war and showed their fighting mettle, for they were fighting for a cause in which they believed and sought death as martyrs to save the Holy Land from the Zionists. Their performance in Palestine made the prime minister of the day, Nuqrashi, conscious of the danger they as a movement represented to the security of the state; it also made some of the military men equally conscious of their fighting skills, as we shall see later. In December 1948 the premier decided to suppress the Muslim Brethren and ordered the dissolution of the Society. By so doing the premier had signed his own death warrant, for three weeks later he was assassinated by one of the Brethren. In turn the leader of the Society, Hasan al-Banna, was assassinated, presumably by someone in the government, in retaliation for the death of the premier.

The Brethren were proscribed; several were arrested, as were many of the socialists and leftists of the time. A series of armistice agreements between the various Arab governments and the Israelis were eventually signed, which brought active fighting to an end. These were not peace agreements – there were none – they brought only a cessation of fighting, for the Arabs refused to recognize the creation of the state of Israel, and even refused to negotiate face to face with the Israelis; the negotiations were carried out by third parties.

The war in Palestine laid bare the bankrupt nature of internal politics in Egypt, and clearly revealed the loss of leadership on the part of any of the political parties, not only the Wafd. Rumours of scandals surrounding the king's private life abounded. He could be seen any evening in one of the popular nightclubs surrounded by a bevy of beauties, or at the gambling tables of the Automobile Club. His divorce of his queen, Farida, was unpopular among the people and his loose behaviour was viewed with disfavour. Gossip raged over the business deals and over the purchase of arms during the war, which involved the king's closest companions and which cost public money. These men included the court electrician, an Italian named Pulli, and a Levantine newspaper man, who amassed fortunes and wielded power through their relationships with the king. Nahhas's wife became the target of gossip when stories circulated that, for a price, she had helped rig the cotton exchange in Alexandria in favour of two of her friends, but had ruined a number of cotton merchants in the process. Every day a new scandal circulated in the salons of Cairo and the coffee houses of the country. The monarchy had by then lost all respect; the government had abdicated responsibility and showed as little moral fibre as the monarchy. Strikes and demonstrations had become commonplace as the cost of living had risen.

In 1950 elections once more returned the Wafd to power and Nahhas sought to deflect attention from internal problems he neither wished to confront nor knew how to solve by trying to reach some settlement with Britain over the Suez Canal and the evacuation of the Canal Zone. While still a genuine political problem, it was once again raised as a red herring to distract attention from the incompetence and corruption of the government. Meanwhile the Sudanese were busy trying to wrest their country's independence from Britain, while the Egyptians were trying to effect a union with the Sudan. Not knowing what to do next, Nahhas in 1951 finally unilaterally abrogated the Anglo-Egyptian Treaty of 1936 and the Sudan Convention of 1899. Parliament promptly declared the monarch King of Egypt and the Sudan, though neither of these moves immediately undermined British control of the Sudan.

Young Egyptians carried out guerrilla attacks against the British bases in the Canal Zone, hoping thereby to make the region untenable for the British army and force an evacuation. But the British army, having lost its base in Palestine, was determined to hang on to the Canal Zone. On 25 January 1952, British army units surrounded a police station in the town of Ismailiyya, believing the police to be aiding and abetting the guerrillas, and demanded their surrender. The Egyptian police, on orders from the minister of the interior, refused to surrender. They were surrounded by tanks and artillery was used against the building, killing forty Egyptian policemen and wounding seventy before the remainder finally surrendered. That was the spark that set off a conflagration that burned down a sizeable part of Cairo. When the news of the events in Ismailiyya reached the capital, on the following day a mob roamed round Cairo setting fire to British-owned establishments, clubs and businesses, and others belonging to foreigners. A pall of black smoke hung over Cairo as people cowered in their houses and watched in fear while an ever growing mob seemed to go berserk as it burnt buildings, looted stores and destroyed property. It was only by the afternoon, when the army had been belatedly called out, that order was restored. By then the centre of Cairo looked like a ravaged war zone with gutted department stores, smouldering buildings and smashed shop fronts.

Who was behind the burning of Cairo? Was it organized or spontaneous? These are questions that remain unanswered to the present day, although speculation is rife. There were rumours that a certain black car was seen going from area to area leading the attacks on specific buildings. The truth will probably never be known but there were strong rumours the events had been organized by Ahmad Husain of Misr al-Fatat, and indeed he was later tried for it but the case was shelved when Nasser came to power. Others claimed the Polish embassy had supplied the sophisticated incendiary materials that were used.

The burning of Cairo, much like the burning of Alexandria seventy years earlier, was a landmark in the history of Egypt. It signified the end of an era, the era of liberal experiment. Parliament had proved ineffective in the face of both the monarch and the political parties and governments of the day. The political parties had run out of imagination and backbone and could only react to, not initiate, events. The monarch was completely discredited both in his personal and in his public life. For six months various palace-appointed regimes tried to limp along, but the *coup de grâce* came on 23 July 1952 when a handful of young officers organized a *coup d'état* that overthrew the monarchy and the form of government that had existed since 1922.

The army had always supported the monarchy and had never interfered in politics, but the war in Palestine had changed all that. A new class of officer had come into existence after 1936 and ten years later the war in Palestine had changed their perception of duty towards their country. Animosity towards the king became apparent on the part of the younger officers and manifested itself during elections for the presidency of the Officers' Club. The king had always looked upon the army as his special favourite, but that feeling gave way to displeasure when his candidate for the presidency was outvoted by an older, more popular general named Muhammad Naguib. It was a message sent to him by his army that they no longer accepted his leadership. From then on king and younger officers were on a collision course. There were various rumours of dissatisfaction among the younger officers, even of attempts at *coups d'état*, so the king asked his minister of defence to look into them. The minister called in his own nephew, a young officer named Abd al-Hakim Amir, and asked him if he had heard of any rumours of disaffection among his young colleagues. Amir, one of the conspirators, reported it was nothing more than a 'storm in a teacup' and the minister reported this view to the king. The following morning a stunned country awoke to hear that the broadcasting station had been occupied by the military, who had organized a *coup d'état* that had ousted the monarchy.

Three days later Faruq left Egypt, accompanied by his second wife, daughters and infant son, who was declared the new king of Egypt under the aegis of a regency council which would rule in his name until he attained his majority. The regency council was composed of Prince Abd al-Munim, a respected member of the royal family, the son of the former Khedive Abbas II, who had been deposed by the British in 1914; Bahi al-Din Barakat Pasha, former state auditor and several times a cabinet minister; and Rashad Muhanna, an army officer. A year later the monarchy was dissolved and Egypt declared a republic with General Muhammad Naguib its first president.

6   The Nasser years, 1952–70

For the first time in over two thousand years, since the days of the Pharaohs, Egypt was ruled by Egyptians. The Turco-Circassian monarchy sustained and bolstered by British guns was gone. At last it seemed the alienation of the ruled from their rulers was to come to an end. The new regime was one with which the majority of native Egyptians could identify in terms of religion, language and ethnicity, the Coptic minority being an exception as far as religion was concerned. Like his grandfather, the monarch was deposed without a voice being raised in his favour.

The loss of the monarchy led many to believe that it also meant the end of British meddling in Egyptian internal politics, for British influence within Egypt was associated with the presence of a king who could dismiss governments when ordered to do so. The advent of nationalists to power, in somewhat the same fashion as the advent of the first government under the Wafd, seemed to inspire a belief that a purely Egyptian government operating for the well-being of Egyptians had been established. Everyone believed the officers were nationalists who wanted to reform the country.

Most of the Free Officers had entered the military academy after the treaty of 1936 had made this possible. Most were members of the same graduating class, had served together in military posts and were friends as well as companions in arms. They had organized early in their careers, while they were still lieutenants, and had deliberately infiltrated every political grouping available so as to learn their techniques and their goals. Thus Nasser and Anwar al-Sadat joined the Muslim Brotherhood, while some joined Misr al-Fatat, and others joined left-wing groups. With only a few exceptions, the members of the original thirteen-man central planning organization, the Revolutionary Command Council, came from the same social milieu – the lower middle and lower classes.

Once they had ousted the monarch, the officers next saw their role to be liberators of Egypt from the British occupation – the ideal that had driven every Egyptian politician from 1919 onwards. Other than that one constant goal, they had no clear idea of what they would do next: whether to seize power from the civilians or allow the civilians to govern under their watchful eye. Although the previous regime had been discredited, liberal government had not. The notion of representative government, of constitutional rule and even of political parties was not discarded; it was the way in which such liberal government had been abused that was discredited. The officers believed the liberal experiment had been manipulated by the British and the monarch and therefore had been doomed to failure because of such manipulation. That was one reason why they had assumed the political parties would soon pull themselves together and collaborate to build a new Egypt. Whether it was disappointment at the backbiting that arose between the parties, as Nasser claimed, that caused disillusion with a liberal form of government, or whether the officers found the lure of power too strong to resist, they soon decided to take an active role in the administration of the country. Officers became instant bureaucrats and cabinet ministers, and had to learn the ropes through experience, sometimes with disastrous results. Meanwhile the experienced politicians were arrested, imprisoned and later forbidden to participate in any political activity.

At first the public assumed there would be an immediate return to parliamentary life, a hope that was soon squashed. A schism had appeared within the ranks of the officers, between those who wanted parliamentary government, and those who, under Nasser's direction, opted for a different form of rule. General Naguib, who had been used as a front by the officers to give respectability to the movement because of his reputation as a senior officer of integrity, and who consequently had been elected the first president of the Egyptian republic in 1953, led the grouping which demanded a return to constitutional life. That grouping was outmanoeuvred by Nasser's faction and, fearing an outbreak of violence between fellow officers, it acceded to the dominant faction. Naguib however soon found himself under house arrest. When Ahmad Lutfi al-Sayyid, a respected elder states-man, refused the offer to become Egypt's second president, Nasser took on the position himself.

On first coming to power the officers had abolished the consti-tution and declared a three-year transitional period while they decided what form of government the country would have. A provi-sional constitution invested the Revolutionary Command Council with full powers and with an organization, the Liberation Rally, which was set up in lieu of political parties. It may be the officers real-ized that if they allowed free elections to take place the old political parties would win the elections with an overwhelming majority, for the officers were as yet an unknown and untried element. Therefore the old politicians were to be discredited, not returned to office. A law limiting land ownership, the source of the wealth and influence of the *ancien régime*, was passed limiting land ownership to 200 faddans per person. While this broke the power and the holdings of some of the larger landowners, it was nevertheless a sizeable holding in a country where the majority of landholders, the fallahin, possessed less than 50 faddans; thus it allowed large families to retain control over vast areas of land by giving 200 faddans to every individual member of the family. Consequently the law was modified a second and a third time in later years to limit land ownership to 50 faddans.

In October 1954 Nasser was the subject of an assassination attempt said to have been organized by the Muslim Brethren. The Brethren had helped the officers come to power and expected a share in the government of the country. But once in power the officers saw no need to associate the Brethren with their government, especially since the Brethren possessed a massive, popular power base, and the officers had no power base as yet. Nasser must have known were the Brethren to be associated with government, they would acquire the potential to displace him and he may therefore have sought to discredit

them. In any event the Society was discredited by that act, was proscribed and went underground, although a few years later it was to
surface once again and to become as powerful as it had been. Nasser
however was never again challenged.

Negotiations with Britain over the evacuation of the Canal
Zone were begun in April 1953. Guerrilla attacks on the army bases
in the Canal Zone had put a tremendous burden on British army personnel. The army needed more men to keep the base in face of popular
opposition within the country, when workers began to boycott the
base. Britain could neither spare the men nor afford the expense of
extra attention to the base. Yet the British government could not see
its way to evacuating the base, so talks were broken off. Talks were
resumed a few months later when an evacuation agreement was
reached and signed in October 1954. The agreement allowed for evacuation of British military personnel from the Canal Zone by June
1956. Protection of the Canal would then become an Egyptian responsibility, and no longer would foreign troops be based on Egyptian soil.
The other main issue, the Sudan, was separated from the Canal issue.

The Sudan was allowed to hold free elections in 1953 and to
undergo a three-year transitional period while the Sudanese decided
what they wanted: whether to join with Egypt or to become independent. Nasser sent Major Salah Salim, one of the Free Officers, to woo
the Sudanese, and he became famous as the 'dancing major' when he
was photographed dancing with some tribesmen, wearing nothing but
his shorts. The British government also wooed the Sudanese and
assured them of support should they opt for independence instead of
union with Egypt, of which they disapproved. The Sudanese opted for
independence in 1956, and Egypt was forced to face the political fact
that the independence they wanted for themselves was also desired
by other peoples.

Once the new regime had succeeded in dominating the
Egyptian scene and in solving its problems with Britain, enhancing its
standing, it turned to the problem of foreign policy in general.
Egyptian politicians had always believed they were the natural

leaders of the Arab world and the Islamic world; the new politicians were no different. Indeed they also believed they should lead the African states as well. That assumption of leadership was soon to bring the governments of Egypt and Iraq onto a collision course.

The cold war between the United States and the Soviet Union had led to the creation by the former of a series of military alliances which John Foster Dulles, the secretary of state, believed would contain the Soviet Union within a ring of alliances and pacts friendly to the United States. Thus the North Atlantic Treaty Organization (NATO) was matched by the Southeast Asia Treaty Organization (SEATO), and by the establishment of the Baghdad Pact between Iraq, Turkey and Pakistan. The Egyptian government refused to join any regional alliance and assumed the British government, a member of the Baghdad Pact, was out to undermine Egypt's regional leadership by shifting the centre of power in the Arab world to Baghdad. The Egyptian government then began a campaign designed to dissuade the Arab states from joining the pact. A new radio station, the Voice of the Arabs, beamed a powerful message to Arab lands, attacking Nuri al-Said, the Iraqi prime minister, as a traitor to the Arab cause, and attacking the collective pact which had been signed in 1950 by the Arabs. The rivalry between Egypt and Iraq for supremacy in leadership of the Arabs had started in the forties with the founding of the Arab League which Iraq hoped to lead, but which had an Egyptian president and headquarters in Egypt.

Iraq was not the only Arab country to be attacked by the new Egyptian regime. Other Arab lands which did not endorse the Egyptian policy with enthusiasm were dubbed 'reactionaries and feudalists' and attacked by the Voice of the Arabs. Animosity was mainly directed towards Saudi Arabia and Jordan.

When the Free Officers first came to power they searched for some trend in foreign affairs they could follow, and found affinity in the politics and policies of President Tito of Yugoslavia and of Pandit Nehru of India. Nehru saw in Nasser a reflection of himself as a young man and advised and guided the new Egyptian leader. Together with

President Sukarno of Indonesia, these leaders called for a conference of neutral or non-aligned countries in Bandung in April 1955. There Nasser was treated as a world leader by the delegates of the Third World and honoured by men of world stature such as Chou En-lai. Bandung was a turning point for Nasser; it made him appreciate the potential for leadership that he had over the Third World, which admired his ousting of a corrupt monarchy and his ability to handle affairs with Britain. This was the era of decolonization when the Third World had just begun to rid itself of colonial rule and to begin to find its way in world affairs. The conference affirmed the Egyptian regime's resistance to colonialism and to the lure of military pacts with the old colonial powers. That position caused the Western bloc, especially the United States, to accuse the members of the conference of hypocrisy and of sitting on a fence in the middle of a cold war. As far as the Third World was concerned, though fence-sitting was not a comfortable position, it was at least safe, and it allowed governments to stay out of quarrels between the two superpowers. It also allowed them to receive financial aid from both sides, who wooed them, hoping to get some commitment from them.

John Foster Dulles was angered by Egypt's participation in the Bandung conference, and by Nasser's prominent role. He took the attitude that whoever was not clearly an ally of the United States was an ally of the Soviet Union. Neutrality, he believed, was nothing but a sham. That attitude was to create difficulties for Egypt at a later stage.

After Bandung, Nasser may have become a leader outside his country, but he was still the *rais* (leader) of a country which could not defend itself against Israeli attacks. The Western powers had placed a moratorium on the sale of arms to the Arab states, especially after the failure of the Baghdad Pact. The only other source of arms lay in the Eastern bloc, which had sold arms to Israel during the war of 1948. Nasser turned to Russia for his weapons, although the sale was ostensibly with Czechoslovakia.

Israel was disturbed by Egypt's independence of Britain, and in 1954 it mounted the Lavon affair. Israeli agents destroyed British and

United States property in Cairo believing the damage would be blamed on Egyptian xenophobia and worsen Egypt's relations with those countries. The affair was discovered and the perpetrators caught and hanged. The government of Israel denied all knowledge of the affair, although the full story was at a later date made public in Israel, and the role of Israeli agents in the Cairo incidents clearly revealed. The following year Ben Gurion came out of retirement on his kibbutz and, as minister for defence, authorized a raid on the Gaza strip which caused the death of a number of Egyptians and Palestinians. The raid graphically underlined the weakness of Egypt's military position and her need for arms. Ben Gurion had ordered the raid out of fear of Nasser's support of the Palestinians and his arming of *fidayyin* (guerrillas). The raid was to be a lesson, or a means of forcing Nasser to reduce support for the Palestinians. And yet at that time Egyptian support for the Palestinians was mostly verbal, for the Egyptians had few weapons to offer anyone, hence the urgency of finding an arms supplier.

The Czech arms deal was successfully negotiated and served to add fuel to the fire of John Foster Dulles's anger with Nasser. During that period the Egyptian government had planned a High Dam project which was believed to be able to double the amount of agricultural land, provide hydroelectric power for industry, and become the symbol of a new resurgent Egypt. The World Bank and the United States government were to be the main financial backers of the scheme. Probably because of pressure from the Jewish lobby, Dulles decided to use the High Dam as the occasion for teaching Nasser and other Third World leaders a lesson. He withdrew United States backing from the project in a most cavalier and public fashion, designed to humiliate Nasser personally, and Egypt, before the world.

In retaliation Nasser nationalized the Suez Canal, and announced he would use the income from the Canal to finance the High Dam. The Canal concession was due to end in 1968, unless it were renewed, and no Egyptian leader would have renewed the concession; the last leader who had talked about renewing the concession in 1911 had been assassinated for even suggesting it. Feelings of animosity harboured by Egyptians towards the Suez Canal concession had not abated, for to most of them the Canal represented European exploitation of native resources of the most blatant sort – an economic imperialism. The nationalization of the Canal was thus greeted with jubilation by most Egyptians.

Anthony Eden, the British prime minister, was affronted at the nationalization of the Canal for personal as well as for political and economic reasons. In the first place the Canal, though a French company, was most extensively used by British shipping. Both Britain and France depended on oil shipped through the Canal for their energy resources, so the Canal was a lifeline and any threat to it represented a direct threat to their industries and well-being. That was a cogent economic reason for both states to decry the nationalization of a waterway they had grown to consider as their own over the past seventy years. Eden had further grievances against Nasser for he had negotiated the Canal settlement with him when he was foreign secretary and believed Nasser had deliberately lied to him and cheated him when he had signed the treaty, and had planned all along to nationalize the Canal when the last British soldier left the Canal Zone. He greeted the news of the nationalization of the Canal with cries of 'theft' and 'blackmail'. Nasser had not lied to Eden, nor do we have any proof he had planned to nationalize the Canal at any time before the High Dam project had been turned down; he had resorted to nationalization of the Canal in retaliation at Dulles's rebuff, and that of the World Bank in refusing to finance a project he looked upon as his brain child, his means of pulling his country out of poverty and into the modern age.

France was equally incensed over the nationalization of the Canal, which was managed by a French company, and designed and built by a French engineer. But France had an added grievance against Nasser. From 1954 France was enmeshed in the Algerian war of independence and the French government suspected the Algerians were aided, financed and trained in Egypt. The French government chose to believe that without Egyptian support the Algerians would have no powerful ally and the revolt would be crushed. That was to underestimate the power of Algerian national feeling, and to overestimate the minimal aid the Egyptian government offered the Algerians.

Israel was equally worried over Nasser's growing stature in the region, and more so by his new supply of weapons, which they thought had been obtained to attack Israel.

When the nationalization of the Canal was made public the Powers at first invited Nasser to attend an international conference to discuss the future of the Canal, for Nasser had set a precedent which could be followed by other Third World countries. However, when Eden attacked Nasser in personal terms and described him as a potential Hitler, Nasser refused to attend the conference. Overnight Nasser became a hero to the Third World for he had snubbed the West and seemed to be getting away with it. Furthermore, to add insult to injury, the allegations made by the former management of the company that the Egyptians would be incapable of managing the Canal and all traffic would come to a grinding halt, were proved wrong. The Egyptian pilots demonstrated they could take convoys of ships through the Canal just as safely and efficiently, but less expensively than the foreign pilots previously hired by the company. For all these reasons, together with Israel, Britain and France launched a tripartite attack against Egypt in October 1956.

The British and the French governments assumed an attack would cause the Egyptians to blame the military regime and rise en masse against them and overthrow the military even before it became necessary to occupy the country. They assumed further they could find a few *ancien régime* politicians who would be happy to lead a new government against the Free Officers in collaboration with the invaders. These calculations proved unfounded, for the people rallied closer to their leader, especially when it rapidly became clear that Israel was a party to the collusion. The attack against Egypt might have been forgiven, or even condoned by some, so long as Israel was not a partner in the act of aggression. The very presence of Israel was a guarantee of popular resistance and a rally round the leader and the army by the entire population.

The Israelis rapidly occupied the Sinai peninsula up to the Suez Canal, while British and French forces destroyed the Egyptian air force, on the ground, bombarded the city of Port Said, and finally occupied it. Resistance in Port Said, though brave, was ineffective against overwhelming odds and the city fell. Casualties on the Egyptian side were high. The United States and the Soviet Union both intervened to stop the fighting and deplored the invasion of Egypt by the three countries. The United States government was adamant that fighting should cease and enemy forces withdraw from all Egyptian territory. A ceasefire was negotiated by the United Nations on 6 November, after a week of fighting, and United Nations Emergency Forces (UNEF) were sent to Egypt to act as a buffer zone between it and Israel. Israeli forces were forced to withdraw to their previous boundaries when the United Nations Emergency Forces landed in Egypt on 22 December.

The Egyptian government claimed they had emerged victorious from that war, or at least if they did not believe they had won the war, they knew they had won the peace. They had stood up to the might of three states and had not been completely defeated by them. The regime had weathered the storm and had not fallen. On the other hand the invasion of Egypt had been so badly bungled by Britain and France that it was little short of humiliating. Had they carried out a swift and efficient occupation, and faced the world with a *fait accompli*, they might have got away with it. But their slow, piecemeal, uncoordinated invasion was so poorly conceived that it roused the criticism of the rest of the world, which despised shillyshallying and incompetence, but might have admired and condoned tough efficiency. When in 1882 the British admiral of the fleet lying off the coast of Alexandria bombarded that city, he explained that it was to 'clear the air'. By 1956 bombardments of countries did not serve the same purpose.

During the war the Canal had been blocked by sinking ships, but it was cleared by the United Nations and opened for traffic in

March 1957. The Canal company was offered compensation and the waterway functioned successfully until 1967 when another Arab–Israeli war once again caused it to be blocked and for a much longer period of time.

As a consequence of the events of 1956, a large number of aliens were deported from Egypt, especially British and French nationals, along with many Jews. A majority of members in the Greek and Italian communities, who had been residents of Egypt for a long time, also left in the wake of the British and French; they felt their economic position in the country was threatened by the rising wave of nationalist feeling. In the past foreign nationals had been 'protected' by the capitulations and by the British presence, and had felt secure with a British army of occupation in the country. A certain cosmopolitanism, especially in the city of Alexandria, had reigned, and aliens had felt welcome and at home in Egypt. With the increase of nationalist feeling, aliens now had to rely on the goodwill of the local government to 'protect' them. Whereas in the past the very fact that they were foreign had been a business asset, it was now a handicap with a government that preferred to deal with Egyptians. Many members of foreign communities thus decided to leave Egypt.

Nasser had emerged from that experience as the undoubted leader of the Arab world and the hero of the populace in all Arab countries, although he was certainly not that to any of the Arab leaders. The Arab peoples admired Nasser for all he represented – unity among Arabs, pride in self, an end to colonial influence, independence. His picture was to be found in every shop and bazaar in all Arab countries. Those who admired Nasser most were perhaps the Syrians.

Since 1949 Syria had undergone a series of military *coups d'état* resulting in dictatorships and was enmeshed in internal problems. A pan-Arab movement, called the Baath (Renaissance) party had been started in the forties by two intellectuals, Michel Aflaq and Salah al-Bitar, and had been gaining ground. Its message was the need to unite all Arabic-speaking countries into one single Arab nation. At first the Baath were inimical to the new regime in Egypt, but when Nasser talked of need for Arab unity, he and the members of the Baath seemed to find common ground. The Baath saw in Nasser a potential leader for the Arabs, while he saw in the Baath a potential ideology that supported his role as the unifier of all the Arabs. The rulers of the other Arab states feared the concept of Arab unity would mean the end of their regimes, especially when Nasser embarked on diatribes against those he called 'feudalists' and 'reactionaries'. The Egyptian regime was not content with diatribes only and in 1957 a number of military attachés were expelled from Arab countries, accused of fomenting disturbances within these countries.

In addition to the Baath movement, Syria was also facing a growing communist current which gave the Syrian non-communist leaders cause for unease. The president of the Syrian Republic, Shukri al-Quwatli, an elderly politician who had been a leader of the nationalist movement against the French occupation of Syria and had been exiled to Egypt by one of the military coups when he got to know Nasser, feared a communist takeover of the army. Together with members of the Baath party, he moved for a union with Egypt to forestall a communist regime in Syria. In January 1958 Nasser was invited, not to say pressured, into a union with Syria as the first step towards an eventual unity of all Arab states. Nasser could clearly see the danger of embarking on such a union without adequate preparation, but could not resist the lure of a first step towards Arab unity, and agreed to the creation of the United Arab Republic. Yemen also joined the union.

The task of merging the political structures of two such disparate entities as Egypt and Syria was begun, but it ended in failure. All political parties, including the Baath, were abolished in Syria, as they had been in Egypt. A new constitution was hastily drawn up and Nasser was elected president of the new republic by 99.9 per cent of the votes. The Syrian social structure was different from the Egyptian, and what may have satisfied one society ran counter to the needs of the other. By then Egypt had become accustomed to authoritarian rule and to a one-party system in which workers and peasants were represented, but which alienated much of the bourgeoisie, which was small in number. Syria, on the other hand, had a highly articulate and effective bourgeois class, and a large segment of the population dealt in craft and small workshop industries as well as in small businesses. The haste with which the union had been effected gave little time for both societies to be studied, and a policy to integrate the two societies and address itself to their needs and problems was not established. Furthermore the Egyptians were accused of ruling Syria with a heavy hand and of failing to grant the Syrians a fair share of positions of power, either in the army or in the civilian administration. In addition a repressive apparatus was set up and Abd al-Hamid Sarraj appointed the head of Syrian military intelligence, a man who became Nasser's man in Syria and ruled the country with a ruthless and unpopular hand.

Many Syrians became disgruntled at their new regime which alienated them from the centres of power and replaced them with Egyptians. Others were soon upset by the socialization decrees which were passed in July 1961 and which turned private businesses into nationalized, state-dominated enterprises. To a nation of entrepreneurs and small businessmen this was too much, too suddenly. The civilians were not the only disgruntled ones, for the army too began to manifest its dissatisfaction with the new government and especially with the Egyptian high command. In a gesture of conciliation Nasser sent Abd al-Hakim Amir, the commander-in-chief of the Egyptian army, and his closest friend and companion, to settle Syrian grievances. Amir, though popular among the military, whose cause he advanced with success, was nonetheless neither an effective leader nor a troubleshooter. Rumours soon spread that he was too busy courting an Algerian singer to pay much attention to what was going on in the country, let alone to try and remedy Syrian grievances. In September 1961 Syrian army units marched into Damascus, roused Amir from his bed and sent him home to Egypt in his pyjamas, accompanied by the singer in question in her nightgown, in a deliberately malicious gesture of ridicule. A national uprising followed and the

Syrians manifested their delight at being rid of what they had called 'the Egyptian occupation'.

Nasser was stunned. The shock soon turned to introspection and a consideration of what had gone wrong, and so to a reorganization of Egyptian internal affairs. His reputation had suffered a setback, but he believed he still had enough stature and credit with his people to survive such a setback, perhaps even to get the Syrians to reconsider their decision. He refused to change the name of the state, keeping it as the United Arab Republic, hoping for a Syrian change of heart. The name of the state allowed the irrepressible Egyptians humour at the rais's expense with a joke that claimed the United Arab Republic signified the union of Upper and Lower Egypt.

The union between Egypt and Syria had been cause for distress on the part of other Arab rulers. The rulers of Jordan and Iraq saw threats to their thrones. In Lebanon Camille Chamoun took an anti-Nasser stand and, shifting to a pro-Western position, he endorsed the Eisenhower Doctrine, which allowed the American government to give military aid to Middle Eastern governments who requested it. This move alienated those Lebanese who supported Nasser and the cause of Arab unity. Chamoun had also manipulated the parliamentary elections of 1957, and tried to push through a constitutional amendment which would allow him a second term as president, which further angered the opposition. Violence broke out and by 1958 civil disorders between pro-Western Maronite Chamoun followers and pro-Arab supporters formed of Druze, Muslims, Greek Orthodox and even some Maronites, including the Maronite patriarch who feared Chamoun's stance would jeopardize the position of Christians in the Arab world. The disorders soon developed into a full-scale civil war. When the war seemed to tilt in favour of the pro-Nasser camp, Chamoun called upon the United States to land marines in Lebanon, according to the terms of the Eisenhower Doctrine, but this did not help the situation much. The civil war soon threatened to ruin Lebanese businessmen of all religious denominations and, when their situation became desperate and Lebanon's economy was threatened with collapse, an alliance of Christian and Muslim politicians with pro-Arab, pro-Nasser sympathies, took power.

In Iraq a crisis was brewing which culminated in a military coup that overthrew the regime, massacred the ruling elite in the most brutal fashion, and established a military dictatorship under General Abd al-Karim Qasim and Colonel Abd al-Salam Arif, an admirer of Nasser. At first Nasser welcomed the new regime in Iraq, which he expected would join the United Arab Republic and enlarge the union, but Qasim refused to be drawn in and remained aloof. He soon got rid of the pro-Nasser Arif, his co-conspirator, and, allying himself to the communists, he suppressed the pro-Nasser faction in a bloody revolt in Mosul in 1959. He soon turned against the communist faction and massacred them, but his relations with Egypt remained acrimonious.

In Yemen a revolution led by anti-royalist army officers broke out and eventually led to the establishment of the republic of North Yemen in 1962. The deposed ruler, the Imam Badr, who had narrowly escaped death, rallied his tribesmen in a counter-revolution, aided by funds and weapons supplied by Saudi Arabia. On the other hand the revolutionaries, led by Abdallah al-Sallal, turned to Egypt for assistance. Egypt, which had been preaching change of regimes, could not avoid lending support to Sallal, who hoped to modernize his country. Nasser however made the mistake of underestimating Yemeni royalist resistance and sent Egyptian forces to Yemen. Had Nasser ever read any history of the region he would have known what a mistake it was to send forces to that country, for no one but a native had ever won a war there. The Egyptian forces became embroiled in a rugged, mountainous terrain that had no roads and was ideal for guerrilla warfare and ambushing. The Imam and his tribesmen inflicted heavy casualties on the Egyptian army, which at one time numbered 70,000 men. That adventure sapped Egyptian funds, slowed the country's economic growth and wasted its scarce resources. It also brought Egypt and Saudi Arabia into open animosity and nearly to the brink of war. The United States, in support of its ally, Saudi Arabia, tried to pressurize Egypt to end the war and alienated Nasser even further, causing him to distrust any further United States attempts at mediation. The opposition between Egypt and Saudi Arabia came to an end in 1967, when Egypt found itself in trouble with Israel.

Up to the 1960s Egypt's economic condition had been improving. Industrialization had been a major plank in the new regime's platform. Prior to the revolution there had been a small industrial sector in the country which produced textiles, processed food and small appliances. The Bank Misr and its affiliates were actively industrializing the country, but 60 per cent of all industry was owned by foreigners. In 1955 the new regime had negotiated for the construction of an iron and steel complex, to be built at Hilwan. The blast furnace cracked and had to be replaced. The project resulted in the waste of a great deal of both time and money. Hilwan was not the ideal site for such a project, being far away from the source of iron ore, but was adopted for political reasons. Eventually the complex produced enough steel to meet most of the demands of the local market. With the aid of manufacturers such as Fiat, car assembly plants were set up. All these projects demanded large amounts of capital and gave, as yet, little in return, though they did supply jobs for workers. Foreign imports which necessitated the expenditure of foreign exchange, a rare commodity, were cut down to a bare minimum while import substitution went on apace. Factories successfully turned out home appliances, stoves, fridges, and waterheaters.

The economic goals that had been set for the country had been unrealistic for they aimed at doubling the gross national product within a decade by means of two five-year plans, only one of which was ever implemented. Land-reclamation projects were equally ambitious and unrealistic. One project started in the desert between Cairo and Alexandria, called the Liberation Province, turned out to be costly, badly managed and riddled with corruption. In spite of these drawbacks, there was a healthy 6 per cent yearly increase in GNP, which boded well for the future. Money was spent lavishly on some projects; others necessitated negotiating loans from abroad, as for instance the High Dam scheme. Loans from Eastern-bloc countries were also negotiated to pay for more military hardware, which the country needed but did not have the funds to pay for.

Shortage of funds was a constant problem for the Egyptian government. The new regime could have taxed the working classes; this would have yielded little and would have alienated the regime's major mass support. It could have taxed the military, who were the major beneficiaries of the regime, or the rest of the population, but it did none of these things. The only section of society that was taxed was the government bureaucrats. There was corruption in high places; large amounts of money were siphoned off and disappeared, and yet no one was ever charged, nor was any high official even dismissed for such acts, suspects were merely transferred to other high government positions. Inefficiency was rampant, people frequently being appointed to tasks for which they were not qualified, on the basis of their loyalty rather than their efficiency. Furthermore, keeping the army content and well armed was also costing a great deal. By the mid-sixties, the era of economic progress was to make way for a period of economic hardship.

In 1961 a new set of economic regulations changed the economic course of the country and redirected it along more socialist lines towards state capitalism. Until now private property, save for land tenure, had been respected, and only property belonging to British and French nationals had been nationalized (after the 1956 war). In 1960 the National Bank was nationalized and the following year the remaining banks were also nationalized, as were all insurance companies and major enterprises. These were all made part of a public sector with 51 per cent government ownership. Employees were given a share of the profits and represented on the boards of the various companies. The maximum amount of land that could be owned by any one person was further reduced from the 200 faddans that had been specified a decade earlier to 100 faddans, and in 1969 was again halved to a limit of 50 faddans. Any income over £10,000 a year was taxed at a rate of 90 per cent; few however reported receiving such incomes, so taxes were never adequately collected, and to this day the tax-collecting agency is rife with corruption, under-staffed, and has little coercive power.

The nationalization decrees were also followed by the seques-tration of properties owned by a small elite of some four thousand people. Since these decrees did not touch the mass of the population, which owned neither land nor shares and had no taxable income, there was little outcry over the decrees, except on the part of those whose property had been sequestered. The sequestration and nation-alization decrees did, however, supply the government with capital, said to reach £100 million, which could be further invested in new industrial projects. Compensation for the nationalized property was paid in state bonds bearing 4 per cent interest over 15 years and up to a maximum of £15,000 per sequestered individual.

Foreign exchange, always in short supply, was dwindling even further. The government was hard put to find funds to meet its needs and had to resort to more borrowing from abroad. The war in Yemen bled the country white and accelerated a cycle of dependency on Eastern-bloc countries for loans. Infrastructure deteriorated for lack of maintenance, while several projects were stopped for lack of funds. The war in 1967 was to destroy Egypt's economic progress further and to wipe out all the economic gains of the past decade.

Internally the political situation had developed in the direction of a one-party system. The Liberation Rally, which had been founded in the early years, changed its name to become the National Union, also a single party, in 1956. A National Assembly was elected the fol-lowing year, but the candidates had to be approved by the government before they could run for office. Many *ancien régime* members were proscribed, as were those whose property had been sequestered or nationalized, or any who were suspected of seeking to form an oppo-sition. Thus the slate contained names of government-sponsored can-didates only. Once the union with Syria had been effected, a new constitution and a new National Union and Assembly came into being. The break-up of the union with Syria once again caused the emergence of a new body, the Arab Socialist Union, which was formed in 1962. A national congress was set up to approve a charter that was finally adopted in 1964. This new body was supposed to derive half its members from among the peasantry and the workers, and was to act as a legislature. It was however extremely limited in its effectiveness and more of a rubber stamp for the government. Many Egyptians felt that all these changes could best be described by the French saying: 'Plus ça change, plus c'est la même chose.' All these changes were window-dressing with no real attempts at mass mobilization or at setting up a genuine representative apparatus. People were manipulated by a small coterie that sought to hold on to its power and its vested interests, did not want to share government or authority with the people, and did not even wish to mobilize the people for fear that sooner or later that mobilization would turn against it. None of these bodies therefore acted in an independent fashion. The major purpose of the Arab Socialist Union was presumably as an instrument of mass participation, but that it failed to become, for the simple reason that the administration sought to manipulate that body rather than give it autonomy. The Arab Socialist Union was used to call out a mob (and that only after paying them), but never to act as the voice of the people.

The major centres of power still resided with the army under the popular leadership of Abd al-Hakim Amir, who cherished and protected his fief and saw to it that it received more than its fair share. Relationships between Nasser and Amir were to become strained during the mid-sixties. Though Nasser did not doubt Amir's unswerving loyalty to his person, he had an eminently suspicious nature and slowly grew to believe that Amir's hold on the army might represent a potential threat to his own position. To balance the army, an intelligence apparatus, the notorious *mukhabarat*, was set up, which spied on citizens, tapped telephones and carried out the arrest of those suspected of being Muslim Brethren, communists or anything else inimical to the government. Though it was presumed to be generally efficient, the mukhabarat sometimes made mistakes, as when they came to arrest an elderly pasha only to find out that he had been dead for ten years, or when they went to the wrong flat and arrested the wrong victim, or arrested a prominent Copt accusing him of being a Muslim Brother. Most of these activities were largely exercises in futility or self-serving actions on the part of the apparatus. The mass of the Egyptian population was solidly behind Nasser and his regime, and the Muslim Brethren or the communists could do little damage in face of the man's overwhelming popularity. The arrests simply served to polarize the country and set one group against the other, their function being to act as a means of keeping the country off-balance, the better to dominate it. Nasser spied on his own associates and even had their houses bugged so he could be kept informed of everything they said and thought. Such paranoia created a fragmented society with several political foci of power, instead of creating a united front, which is what the country mostly needed. It created an atmosphere of mutual suspicion and distrust on the part of all the people, whether in government or out of it.

Relations with the United States were deteriorating, especially after the marines landed in Lebanon in 1958 and when sophisticated military equipment – such as Hawk missiles – were delivered to Israel when there was an embargo against delivering such weapons to the Arab countries. By then there was talk that Israel had developed a nuclear capacity. In 1966 Egypt and Syria, in spite of their former differences, joined in a defensive military pact that worried the Israelis. A number of border clashes between Syrians and Israelis awakened feelings of imminent conflict with Israel once again, and Egyptian and Syrian troops massed on their respective frontiers.

To add fuel to the fire, the Russian embassy warned the Egyptians that the Israelis were massing troops on the Syrian border and were preparing first to invade Syria and then to invade Egypt. The Russian information, which was incorrect, was probably fed them by Israeli intelligence sources. Arab states like Syria also played a part in bringing about the war by needling Nasser, accusing him of hiding behind the barrage of the United Nations Emergency Forces. The Israelis sought to provoke a war with the Arabs at a moment when they felt militarily superior, fearing the tables might be turned on them in the future. In May 1967 Nasser, thinking to bluff his way out of a confrontation, requested the withdrawal of the United Nations Emergency Forces from the region of Sharm al-Shaikh, the point at which the borders of Jordan, Saudi Arabia, Egypt and Israel meet on the Red Sea, and closed the Straits of Tiran to Israeli shipping. This act was considered *casus belli* by the Israelis.

Nasser's military advisers urged him to strike first against Israel, but he refused, and at the urging of both the United States and the Soviet Union he publicly announced that he would not be the first to move against the enemy, was ready to negotiate through the intermediary of the United States, and was prepared to send a delegate to negotiate with the government in Washington. King Hussein of Jordan landed in Egypt late in May and signed a defence agreement with Egypt, so the stage was set for a military confrontation, should the need arise, between the three Arab states and Israel.

All through these events Nasser believed he would be able to bluff his way out of a military confrontation and win without firing a single shot. He therefore refused to listen to his commander-in-chief, who requested the regiments from Yemen be recalled, for these were the only troops that had seen military combat, but Nasser disagreed and sent raw recruits to the front as part of his bluff. On 5 June Israel carried out a pre-emptive strike against Egypt that wiped out the air force on the ground. Without air cover the army and the entire country was wide open to the Israeli army, which rapidly overwhelmed Egyptian forces in Sinai and once again reached the shores of the Suez Canal. The Golan heights in Syria and the West Bank in Jordan were also occupied.

Three-quarters of the Egyptian air force was destroyed, while 12,000 men were killed. The army resisted fiercely, but it was not up to par, especially since it lacked air cover. The gap between the soldiers, who were peasants with little training or technical knowledge, and their officers, showed in the field. To make matters worse, during the previous year Shams Badran, who had been Nasser's *chef de cabinet* and had become minister for defence, had shifted many officers into more lucrative civilian positions. In an attempt to build up a network of clients owing him patronage, Badran had settled many of the officers in civilian sinecures for which they were ill-fitted, but where loyalty counted for more than competence. When the war broke out many officers had to be recalled in a hurry and put in command of units they had left some time ago. The last straw was that year the military budget had been cut.

The debacle destroyed the army's morale and roused its resentment. They grew to believe that they had been used by Nasser to play a game of *realpolitik* which had failed, and they were taking the blame for it. The defeat of 1967 was the beginning of the end for Nasser. Egypt and he were shocked at the events which were even more traumatic than the invasion of 1956 had been. Not knowing what to do, Nasser resigned. Within minutes of his resignation the masses surged into the streets of Cairo in a demonstration that was to a large extent spontaneous, although some part of the mob may have been paid to demonstrate. The masses demanded that Nasser withdraw his resignation and remain in power. The general feeling motivating the demonstrators was not so much a sense of loyalty to the person of the rais as a feeling of despair: 'You got us into this mess, now you get us out of it.' Nasser withdrew his resignation, but the old image had been shattered. The victorious charismatic personality that had challenged the mighty West was gone.

Internally Nasser's position was similarly weakened and he believed himself challenged by his closest friends. His first reaction was magnanimously to shoulder the blame himself; then he rapidly passed it on to the army and the air force. Abd al-Hakim Amir, Nasser's closest and oldest friend, resigned his post as commander-in-chief of the army in protest, as did several members of the high command. Speaking out for the first time, Amir called for the freedom of the press, which up until now had been heavily censored, for a more democratic form of government, and for the formation of opposition parties. He called for a halt to socialist policies and emphasized the need to withdraw from too close a relationship with the Soviet Union. Nasser, who had put several air force generals on trial for dereliction of duty, feared that Amir was conspiring with other army generals to oust him from power. Indeed there were strong rumours in the army that Amir had disowned Nasser's actions and had blamed him for not recalling the army units from the Yemen. In consequence, Amir and the army felt betrayed and maligned for being made scapegoats, and may well have been planning a move against Nasser. Before Amir could move, Nasser put him under arrest for conspiring against him and two weeks later a shocked country read in the papers that Amir had committed suicide. Few believed the claim of suicide and a strong belief persisted that the man had been assassinated on the rais's orders.

The courts convicted two of the air force generals of negligence and acquitted the others. Popular reaction was instant and violent. People felt the trials had been a farce, a mockery of justice, and both students and workers took to the streets in demonstrations. The students occupied the university at Cairo and organized sit-ins. Both students and workers demanded the abolition of the Arab Socialist Union and demanded a free assembly and vast internal reforms. Nasser placated them by calling for a new plan of action, which sounded fine on paper, but was never implemented; still, it helped abate the turmoil.

The most interesting post-defeat social phenomenon was the apparition of the Virgin Mary said to be hovering over a small church in a remote suburb of Cairo. The Virgin holds a special place in the hearts of all Egyptians, Christian or Muslim – perhaps as an atavistic throwback to the goddess Isis or simply because she is the symbol of motherhood. Those who saw the apparition claimed it was swathed in a blue light, others claimed to see the image of a woman wrapped in a mantle and carrying a baby. Thousands of Egyptians lined up outside the church every night until the small hours of the morning, hoping to catch a glimpse of the Virgin. Men and women who had lost sons, husbands and fathers during the war sought solace in the apparition.

Miraculous cures were reported. The Socialist Union organized seating in front of the church and charged a fee so people could wait for the apparition in comfort. A wave of religious fervour swept the country. Coptic monasteries, which had been closing down for lack of candidates, now had waiting lists, and such long ones that they would only admit university students. Koran study groups mushroomed among all classes of society, who turned to religion for consolation. Even the rais explained the defeat as God's will.

The message was clear. In spite of the defeat God was still on the side of the Egyptians and had sent the apparition as a consolation. At least that was the way in which the population interpreted the apparition. Religious reform, along with other reforms, was necessary, and there was a palpable return to the study of matters religious and a visible resurgence of religious groups.

From 1967 onwards Egypt's economic situation deteriorated rapidly. Having lost 80 per cent of its military hardware, the country was forced to look for funds to restore its equipment, and the Saudis generously footed the bill. The animosity between that state and Egypt over the Yemen came to an end in these more tragic circumstances, especially when the withdrawal of Egyptian forces from the Yemen was finally negotiated. As a further means of raising cash to pay the interest on the old loans taken out by Egypt, the private sector was encouraged to produce more commodities for export. That measure helped to pay off some of the interest owing, but it also sowed the seeds for the eventual open-door policy that Sadat (Nasser's vice-president and successor) was to introduce at a later date.

An armistice agreement was negotiated with Israel and supplemented by United Nations Resolution 242, which pronounced the 'inadmissibility of territory acquired by force' and reaffirmed the principle of territorial integrity. It called upon Israel to withdraw from 'territories occupied'. The term used in the English translation was left ambiguous, talking of 'territories' not specifying 'all territories' or 'the territories'. Israel therefore refused to withdraw and quibbled over the meaning of the term 'territories', claiming it did not imply all the territories recently occupied. Egypt accepted the resolution, as eventually did all the other Arab countries, but Israel did not move from her position. In consequence, the political stalemate was augmented by a so-called 'war of attrition' between Egypt and Israel, with the latter carrying out deep penetration raids into Egypt, aiming at military, but also civilian, targets, until the Soviets supplied Egypt with ground-to-air missiles and sent Soviet pilots to defend Egyptian air space. A situation of 'no war, no peace' was established. In return for Soviet assistance, Nasser allowed the Soviets a naval base in the Mediterranean.

In July 1970, Egypt and Israel finally accepted a temporary ceasefire and tried to work out a settlement. This temporary halt in violence precipitated an outbreak of hijackings carried out by the Popular Front for the Liberation of Palestine, who tried to attract world attention to the plight of the Palestinians. King Hussein, fearing such activities might endanger his throne, directed his army against Palestinian refugee camps in Jordan and devastated them in what became known as 'Black September'. Nasser was forced to step in and attempt to negotiate between the Palestinians, notably the Palestine Liberation Organization and King Hussein. He succeeded in negotiating refuge for the Palestinians in Lebanon and bringing the blood-letting to an end. The effort involved in carrying out this solution took its toll. Nasser was already a very sick man; he suffered from diabetes and from arteriosclerosis in his leg. Few Egyptians knew the real state of his health, for he flew to Russia for treatment, but the Russian doctors had warned him to avoid tension – impossible advice to follow at this juncture. In September of that year, two days after the summit meeting that settled the Palestinian issue, he suffered a massive heart attack and died.

The death of the president was as traumatic to the Egyptians as the defeat had been three years earlier. A massive and spontaneous outbreak of sorrow swept the country. His funeral procession, which in Muslim countries is organized at the latest on the day following the death, brought out the largest mass of people in any funeral – four million mourners according to the Guinness Book of Records – who demonstrated grief at the death of their leader, and despair over the future of their country. The hero had died, leaving behind him a country partly under foreign occupation, and facing overwhelming problems. If the hero had had feet of clay, at least he had been larger than life, a true colossus who had dominated the Middle East for nearly two decades and caused it to follow the beat of his drum.

The Free Officers had brought parliamentary rule in Egypt to an end, accusing it of corruption and incompetence. It is true the parties of the day and their politicians were incompetent, and a small minority were even corrupt. But parliamentary life had also failed because of the defects of the system, a flawed constitution, the role played by the king, and that played by the British as well. When the Free Officers wiped the slate clean by ousting the king and negotiated the evacuation of the country by British forces, they earned the gratitude and admiration of their people.

The new regime had nationalized property, but that property had belonged to a small elite which had controlled the economy of the country for a century and a half and had done little to improve the lot of the peasant or the worker. Stripping the privileges of ten thousand families at most had probably gladdened the hearts of millions of Egyptians. The exploitation of the poorer classes by the richer did not cease under Nasser and his regime, but the worker and the peasant at least reaped some benefits and gained some material advantages under the new regime. There is little doubt the regime was repressive; it imprisoned people on flimsy charges and held them without trial; it tortured and killed people in jails, abused and humiliated others, but it also gave the rest of the population pride in themselves and in their country, a sense of worth and of dignity.

Under Nasser a new elite had arisen to displace the *ancien régime* which came from among the more underprivileged classes of society. The change therefore benefited the lower and lower-middle classes. New ideologies were introduced, socialism and state ownership of resources, which conflicted with the older ideologies of capi-

THE NASSER YEARS 153

talism and private enterprise. Both old and new ideologies existed side
by side in a public and a private sector. During the following decade
they were to struggle for supremacy. In brief, the new regime, though
it did not allow the population a share in government, allowed them
the semblance of participation. Claiming to act in the name of the
people while directing policies hatched by a small group of bureaucrats, it nonetheless allowed the people to believe they were partici-
pating in decision-making.

Nasser's charisma was the prime reason behind the acquiescence of the masses in his regime. When he talked to the people in the
dialect of Cairo, instead of in the more formal classical language, he
allowed the man in the street to identify with him. His slogan, 'We are
all Nasser', found a responsive echo in the heart of his people. His
personal magnetism did for him what no rational, commonsense
approach taken by any other leader could have done. Egyptians could
either hate him or love him, but they could not remain indifferent to
him, and even those who hated him admitted his stature. On the other
hand, Nasser and his regime set up few institutions that were long-
lasting. Certainly the one-party system was worthless, a rubber stamp.
Press freedom was non-existent; the mass media a tool of the administration. Freedom to dissent was strictly limited, so all opposition
was forced underground. The repressive apparatus of the state was the
main tool of government. Corruption on a larger scale came in. In the
fifties several cases of abuse of authority and blatant embezzlement of
funds had appeared, cases of criminal mismanagement of companies
abounded and members of the new elite were implicated in them. Few
cases were followed through, however, and charges were usually
dropped, for loyalty mattered more to the bureaucracy than anything
else. A law entitled 'Where did you get this from?' was passed in 1958
to judge cases of sudden wealth that was unaccounted for, but again
the guilty were seldom brought to justice. While both Nasser and
Sadat disassociated themselves from corrupt practices, they both condoned them as a means of cementing alliances, acquiring support,
winning opponents and rewarding friends and allies. But worse than

corruption was the lack of continuity built into the government system. The bureaucracy had been personalized by the regime. People were not appointed to positions of authority by any known rule, but through personal connections with others in power and by virtue of their loyalty to the regime. While the normal bureaucracy went through the motions of administration, the real administration was carried out through exceptional decrees, through patron–client relationships, through appeals to individuals in power. Who you knew in power was of greater consequence than the merits of a case. Rule by vested interests, or even by caprice and whim, was more often the case than rule by law and by justice. Several centres of power had grown and had almost become institutionalized. The military represented one focus of power, for in the final analysis the regime was maintained only so long as the military acquiesced in its form of government. The other focus of power was the intelligence apparatus which dominated all other agents of repression. Through its repressive powers it also dominated the bureaucracy. A third focus of power lay with the president's *chef de cabinet* and those men who were closely connected with that office, for they could always speak in the name of the rais. Whether or not the rais had in fact given the orders was unquestioned, so the influence of his cabinet grew to rival the other foci of power. The individuals heading these various organizations saw themselves as the real power centres. They had the ear of the president, and the country was ruled by one man and his apparatus.

In spite of all the mistakes Nasser had made, nevertheless he stands as the only ruler of Egypt who did anything for the mass of the population, notably the poorer, working classes. He created a welfare state that raised the living standard of millions of Egyptians who, to the present day, adulate Nasser and look back to his regime with nostalgia.

Once the rais was dead, who was to become the new rais? None of Nasser's successors had his powerful personality, none controlled any centre of power to the exclusion of others, so internecine quarrels were expected. Anwar al-Sadat, the vice-president of the republic, automatically succeeded the rais, but few expected him to last long for he had the reputation of being a lightweight with no backing who was not to be taken seriously. There were several candidates vying for power, but Sadat, who had survived eighteen years of Nasser when all the other Free Officers had been dismissed or had resigned, was cleverer than his opposition and rapidly arrested the opposition before it could move against him. All police files, telephone taps and repressive measures were to end, he announced to the public; from now on he would govern in a liberal fashion, and seek closer ties with the West. The de-Nasserization of Egypt was to begin.

7   From Sadat to Mubarak, 1970 to the present day

The Cairenes invented a story about Sadat that epitomized the differ-ence between his form of government and that followed by Nasser. The story goes that on the first day Sadat got into the presidential lim-ousine he waited until the car reached a crossroads and then asked the chauffeur, 'Where did the rais turn here?' 'He turned left', was the answer. 'Signal left and turn right', said Sadat. Sadat believed the only way out of the morass of a foreign occupation of Sinai was to turn to the West, and especially to the United States, and get the American government to put pressure on the Israelis to evacuate Arab territo-ries. When talk seemed to lead nowhere he determined to break the deadlock by a limited invasion of Sinai, which could change the situ-ation and lead to negotiations that would, he believed, end in the evacuation of Egyptian territory. From 1971 he announced to the people that this was the year of decision. As the year went on and nothing was decided, the people greeted his statements with derision and claimed the new rais had changed the calendar and doubled or tripled the number of days in the year.

Meanwhile that year, after the Israelis had shot down thirteen Syrian jets, Sadat had a mini summit meeting with King Hussein of Jordan and President Hafiz al-Assad of Syria. Together they agreed to move against Israel. From that time on Egyptian and Syrian officers planned a coordinated attack against Israel to regain occupied territo-ries.

The Saudis had footed the bill for rearming the forces and the Russians supplied them with ground-to-air missiles, the famous arsenal of SAMs. More importantly, Soviet personnel trained the Egyptian army in the use of the weapons and their pilots manned the jets which stopped the Israeli raids into Egypt. Suddenly, in July 1972,

Sadat announced that he had asked all Soviet personnel to leave Egypt. This came as a blow to the army, for though the Russians were unpopular, it nevertheless needed their technology and training. Worse still, when they left the Russians took with them electronic surveillance equipment and jamming devices that were vital to Egyptian defence.

Sadat's reasons for such a move remain unknown, but speculation claimed that he hoped the American government would help him and so dispense with the need to go to war with Israel. When the American government offered nothing in return for having ousted the Soviets, Sadat had to return to his original plan for a limited war. The rest of the year was spent mending fences with the Soviets so they would continue to supply Egypt with weapons.

The critical day came in October 1973 during the Muslim holy month of Ramadan, when all Muslims fast from sunrise to sunset. This coincided with the Jewish Day of Atonement, Yom Kippur. The Israelis did not take Egyptian preparations seriously, for they were convinced they were unbeatable and had so cowed the Arabs that none would dare to attack them. Striking simultaneously, Egyptian and Syrian forces quickly overran Israeli positions and an incredulous world witnessed early Arab victories and an Israeli army in disarray. One Israeli even reported that Moshe Dayan, in tears, suggested surrender.

While the war destroyed the myth of Israeli invincibility, it did not mean victory for the Arabs, for part of the Israeli forces broke through the Egyptian lines and encircled the Third Army. Both superpowers airlifted weapons to their clients, while the United Nations ordered a ceasefire on 22 October, sixteen days after the fighting had started. The Israelis disregarded the ceasefire for several days and clearly ended by winning the war militarily. But the crossing of Suez and the taking of the Bar Lev line was a symbolic victory for the Arabs. It showed they were catching up with Israel militarily and technologically; they might not lose the next round.

Later on some Egyptian generals accused Sadat of having stopped them from pushing their initial military advantage right into

Israel. Some believed that Sadat had promised the American government he would go no further than a certain distance into Sinai, that he wanted to break a stalemate, not destroy Israel. Others claimed the Egyptian advance was stopped when Israel threatened a nuclear strike against the High Dam. Rumours flew high and wild.

The Arabs emerged from the war with a feeling of satisfaction. Arab oil states had imposed an oil embargo, which, while ineffective and doing little damage to the West as far as the flow of oil was concerned, was built up by the oil companies into a major issue. What did damage some Western and Eastern economies was the subsequent increase in oil prices, initiated by the Shah of Iran and followed by the other oil producers. Petro billions flowed into oil-producing countries and consequently the Shah was able to buy arms and equip himself for his role as policeman of the area, a role suggested to him by Kissinger. Arab oil-producing countries also began to buy arms.

After the war Sadat's image within Egypt and the Arab world changed; he became treated with respect as a worthy leader. Gone was the early assessment of Sadat as a lightweight; he was now a rais in his own right.

The war of 1973 may have broken through the stalemate with Israel but it did not bring back Sinai any more than it settled the Palestine issue, another avowed goal of the war. In 1974 an agreement, the outcome of Kissinger's shuttle diplomacy, was signed. The Israelis withdrew to a few miles east of Suez and from a part of the Golan Heights, obliterating the town of Qunaitra before they returned it to the Syrians. Sadat threw his lot in with the Americans and repeatedly said that they held 99 per cent of the cards for peace. He renounced the treaty of friendship he had signed with the Soviets, who stopped supplying him with arms or spare parts. The Egyptian army's arsenal of arms progressively deteriorated, as the Americans had not as yet supplied it with weapons, although they were to do so after Camp David.

From his first days in power Sadat had decided to forgo Nasser's state socialism in favour of a return to a freer form of economy more akin to capitalism. This trend had started during Nasser's last days and Sadat accelerated it. While the public sector still remained, it was slowly being reduced in favour of free enterprise. Nasser's supporters had been the working classes and the intellectuals; Sadat turned to the bourgeoisie, who responded with alacrity. The bourgeoisie was encouraged to expand private enterprise and rapidly developed a class of entrepreneurs and compradors. The government and the new elite hoped to attract Western capital and technology and use it in alliance with Arab capital and cheap Egyptian labour to improve the country's economic condition. The attempt at attracting investment capital was not successful. Few multinational corporations cared to invest in Egypt when another war with Israel might destroy such investments. Some Arabs did invest funds in Egypt to build luxury apartment houses, but this was non-productive investment which generated little employment of a permanent nature and caused inflation. The regime believed that, were peace to come to Egypt, then Egypt could become a haven for multinational corporations just as Taiwan, Singapore and South Korea had. It could thus be argued that Sadat had initiated the October War to make Egypt safe for the economic policy of *infitah* (open-door) as opposed to the previous closed-door policy of protectionism, import substitution and state capitalism, as well as in order to regain Sinai.

Meanwhile Egypt's foreign debt was growing and the country could not meet its interest payments. A large proportion of foreign aid coming from the United States was spent on food subsidies so little was invested in long-term projects that could help the economy. The International Monetary Fund suggested the government stop the subsidies and use the funds more productively. In January 1977 the government announced it would no longer pay the subsidies and instant food riots broke out in Cairo. People went on a wild rampage, burning nightclubs – the signs of affluence and of foreign presence – expensive cars and shouting slogans against Sadat and the members of his family. The riots could only be put down when the army was called in. These events drew attention to the economic plight of the average Egyptian where a few piastres' difference in his budget could spell the difference between eating and starving. At the same time the events persuaded Sadat that he must take a more radical step, that of going to Jerusalem and negotiating with Begin and the Israeli cabinet as a way out of the impasse.

The visit to Jerusalem amazed the world, which credited Sadat with courage and wisdom for undertaking such a step. The visit was explained to the Egyptian masses as necessary before peace and prosperity could be established. Peace with Israel was greeted with enthusiasm by the man in the street, who had been exhausted physically and economically by a series of wars that seemed never to end. There was hardly an Egyptian family that had not lost a son during one war or another; peace and an end to the Palestine issue was heady news indeed. The visit to Jerusalem was followed by the Camp David accords signed in September 1978. These accords alienated Egypt from the Arab world. The Arabs had waited to see the outcome of the visit to Jerusalem before pronouncing on it; they had believed Sadat when he said he was not negotiating a separate peace and that he was hoping for a much more all-embracing settlement. Camp David showed that Sadat had indeed negotiated for nothing more than a separate peace in order to regain Sinai, and Egypt was therefore ostracized from the Arab League and from relations with the Arab world.

Many in Egypt disapproved of the Camp David accords. They believed that, had Sadat been more astute, had he listened to his advisers, he would have gained much, but in his desire to retrieve Sinai he had conceded too many points to the Israelis. They were distressed at the concessions made and saw little reason for haste and for such generosity on the part of Egypt. They were especially distressed over the clauses which set up the exchange of ambassadors and the 'normalization' of relations between the two countries, before all other points had been settled. They disapproved of the clauses dealing with the Palestinians, which shelved the issue rather than settled it. Thus, while planeloads and busloads of Israelis visited Egypt daily, few Egyptians flew to Israel, and fewer still would receive any Israeli socially except under government pressure. In spite of such feelings of antagonism, the fact remained that Egypt had signed a peace treaty with Israel, a treaty that excluded Egypt from the hostile states, leaving the rest of the Arab world much the weaker for having lost their principal fighting force. From then on, the Israelis became more intransigent and belligerent towards the other Arab states and towards the inhabitants of the West Bank.

Both the open-door policy and the Camp David accords were to arouse political animosity towards the Sadat regime. The open-door policy had brought rampant inflation and consequent hardship to those among the population who lived on fixed incomes, such as the mass of the bureaucracy and the military. At the same time it had brought to prominence a new compradorial class which thrived, creating immense wealth, which it spent on conspicuous consumption. After years of austerity under Nasser, consumerism went wild with Paris models and electronic toys filling shop-windows. It also allowed large numbers of blue-collar workers to emigrate to oil-rich countries and enabled those who were left behind to make higher wages as a result of the scarcity of craftsmen and artisans. Professionals also flocked to oil-rich countries, and a new phenomenon occurred, that of fallahin going abroad to work on construction projects.

Officially some two to three million Egyptians were estimated to be working abroad. Unofficially the number was much higher. Egyptians working abroad were estimated by the government to remit some two billion dollars every year. Many scholars have maintained that figure to be in fact less than a tenth of the actual figure. Much of that money, and any other funds coming into the country, were seldom invested productively, but spent on luxury products or on consumer goods. Fallahin invested in land and the price of land rocketed. The number of luxury high-rise apartments grew rapidly, while middle- and lower-income housing was totally neglected. Local goods disappeared from the shops to make way for more expensive foreign imports. The bourgeoisie encouraged the growth of shops and restaurants which featured foreign goods and foods. For example, places selling fast food, of the type sold in the United States, but which to the average Egyptian seemed to be at exorbitant prices, blossomed, while local shops found little custom. It seemed that Westernization, interpreted as consumerism, was sweeping the country with the blessing of the government and its president.

There was certainly a great deal of money flowing into the country after 1977. For one thing, the United States gave Egypt a subsidy of two billion dollars a year, all of which subsidized staple food to avoid a recurrence of the riots of 1977. Oil was discovered in respectable quantities, so Egypt became an oil producer and satisfied the country's own needs as well as exported $2 billion dollars' worth of oil. The Suez Canal and tourism each brought in a further two billion dollars. Yet the government could not balance its budget and depended on remittances from Egyptians abroad. Thus affluence existed side by side with abject poverty and there was a growing gap between the new rich, said to number 27,000 millionaires, and the poor.

There was also political discontent. The liberal regime that had been promised did lift censorship from the mass media for a while, but it was once again restored to suppress any criticism of the president and his actions. Political platforms *(manabir)* had been formed as the first step towards creating political parties, which soon came into existence. However, the parties which disagreed with government policies were censored, and their presses periodically vandalized or shut down. When the New Wafd Party, under Fuad Sirag al-Din, an *ancien régime* politician, criticized Sadat's policies, it was proscribed. The Assembly was only allowed to agree with government measures, or to show opposition in ways which suited the president. As Sadat became more famous on the international scene he seemed to lose touch with his own people. Seeing himself as the father of a family, Egypt, he brooked no opposition nor even discussion of his actions. He seldom consulted his cabinet, or consulted them and then acted contrary to their advice. The same treatment was meted to the military and the foreign office. When criticism of his actions, and the actions of the members of his family and their in-laws, was expressed, he made the Assembly pass a law making it a crime to attack his policies or those of his close associates. That noto-rious 'Law of Shame' even made it illegal for Egyptians abroad to voice opposition to the government. That law was used in 1981 to arrest a mixed group of people and throw them into jail. Among those arrested were members of Muslim militant groups, feminists such as Dr Nawal al-Saadawi, whose sole crime was to attack male domination in the country, Hasanain Haikal, a noted journalist, other journalists, intellectuals and university professors. The arrest of 1,500 people shocked the country, especially when it was followed by a diatribe in which Sadat said he had a list of a further 15,000 names.

Little by little the adulation that had greeted Sadat's actions in 1973 and 1977 turned to contempt for his style of life and that of his kin, for his indifference to public opinion and for his neglect of his Arab brethren in favour of closer ties with the United States and Israel. Had the Israelis been more generous towards Egypt and the Palestinians, had Begin not been so intransigent, Sadat might have kept some of the glitter on his image.

On coming to power Sadat had freed the Muslim Brethren from prison and had made them his allies against the Nasserite ideology then current. Sadat encouraged the growing religious current in the country, hoping to use it for his own purposes; in doing so he helped create a movement that he neither understood nor controlled. Rising religious fervour can be traced back to 1967 among both Muslims and Copts. The defeat in the war with Israel, the appearance of the Virgin were part of a rising religious fervour. Religious associations had found new adherents among the young as well as the old, within the universities and in all walks of life. A visible difference in the mode of dress of people in the street had appeared. Women took to wearing long gowns with long sleeves and a head veil highly reminiscent of a nun's habit. The men also adopted a more modest garb than the open shirts, tight pants and gold chains that were current attire. Little by little Islamic organizations began to show opposition to the

Westernizing currents that swept the country after 1977. The Muslim groups became a genuine opposition, except that their opposition was couched in traditional terms. There is little doubt that Sadat ruled as autocratically as had Nasser, although with a much lesser degree of repression. At the same time opposition was silenced, so the normal channels by which citizens could express their discontent were blocked. Many rallied to the religious groups as an outlet for expressing discontent and demanding changes in government. At the same time the religious groups were expressing a rejection of Westernization, though not of modernization; they were expressing their rejection of the open-door policy and its consequences, and of the results of peace with Israel, and above all deploring the corruption that had invaded government at all levels, especially the highest.

Further disaffection towards the government and its policies developed with the blows that Israel consistently dealt the Arabs: blowing up of the nuclear reactor in Iraq, a series of bombing raids over Lebanon which culminated in the occupation of that unfortunate country, increased settlements on the West Bank and the abuse of the resident Palestinians. Many Egyptians saw these events as a direct consequence of the Camp David accords which permitted the Israelis a free hand while inhibiting Egyptian protest, or action, out of fear that the Israelis might not evacuate the rest of Sinai in April 1982. The Muslim groups viewed such actions as a punishment from God for becoming enmeshed with the foreigners. They believed that only a return to their traditions and religious values could restore an equitable government, one that eschewed corruption and the abuse of power, the hallmark of the regime, and one that kept its distance from the West and acted in its own interests, not according to the dictates of the West.

A large variety of religiously inspired associations arose. Some were politically motivated, forming an opposition group to the party in power. All used religious idiom as their means of communicating criticism of the government and of its cultural baggage. These groups can best be described as alternative groups seeking to supply elements lacking in society such as ideals, means of popular mobilization, curbs to corruption. In brief they posited a holistic approach to society where religious principles became the ideology for behaviour in all activities whether involving man's relationship with his God or man's relationship with man. While these groups were exiguous and totally separate from each other, nonetheless they represented a new rising current of religious activism. One can roughly divide them into two kinds: those who accepted the value system of society and merely sought to reform corruption, and hoped to do so by becoming involved in the political life of the country through party participation; others rejected the value system of society and sought to destroy it and so raise a new system in its place. They are somewhat similar to modern-day anarchists. These are the ones who resort to violence and assassinations to attract support and attention. Their interpretation of what is religiously correct differs from that of the majority of Muslims. Furthermore what they hoped to institute as government has never been explained, nor developed. They talked in simplistic terms and seemed to have a naive view of government and institutions. Some scholars have described the general phenomenon of activist Islam as the revolt of the masses. Where nationalist movements were revolts of the bourgeoisie attempting to wrest rule from colonial authority, the military coups which succeeded them were attempts by the petite bourgeoisie to break away from the domination of the bourgeois, while the activist currents were the revolt of the masses against the exploitation of the two previous classes.

Sadat erroneously believed that these groups were imitating Khomaini and the Iranian revolution, and refused to see that they were a purely internal problem bred by internal issues and inequities. The militant minority believed that those who were not with them were against them, and should no longer be treated as Muslims, but must be executed as unbelievers corrupting the Muslim polity. The arrest of 1,500 citizens galvanized the radical groups into action. During a military parade some radicals managed to break the security ring that surrounded Sadat and, during a moment when attention was drawn to a jet display, they rushed to the grandstand and shot him dead.

While Sadat's assassination moved the United States government and its people as though it had lost one of its own, it barely moved the Egyptians. Sadat had indeed rendered the United States and Israel an immense service when he had signed a peace treaty with Israel. The press in America glorified Sadat and censored any hint of opposition expressed by his own people, so his assassination came as a great blow to the American public, who wept for the loss of their man in Egypt. The Egyptians, a people who are not ashamed of expressing their emotions in public, shed not a tear for the departure of their leader. The delirium that greeted the death of Nasser, who had lost wars and allowed his country to become invaded by a foreign occupier, but was regarded as a true Egyptian, was matched by indifference for the death of a leader who had brought peace to the country and regained the conquered territories, but who had become too closely identified with the West. That is one of the major ironies of history.

Both Nasser and Sadat ruled as autocrats, with a personal style and without any institutions that were either effective or long-lasting. Both of them ruled with the support of a small group of people who carried out their bidding, but who also managed to extend patronage by virtue of their positions, and developed a network of clients. The apparatus round the president ruled on behalf of a small group and their vested interests, regardless of whether by so doing they were harming or benefiting the country. That personal style of government, which is basically rule by caprice (though it is sometimes even the result of rational thought), allowed for no opposition and created no overt and recognizable channels for communication with the population. Opposition then had to be carried out in indirect fashion, through traditional channels, or through personal connections. Such a system encourages government to function through exceptional decrees, and undermines the rule of law and of justice. No matter what the individual merits of an autocrat are, it is the essence of such a government to be personal and lacking in continuity. It is a government of yes-men or men whose advice is seldom sought and frequently overlooked, so that rapid changes of ministers are the norm. Finally it is a government that exerts a certain degree of repression, which in turn calls forth violent reaction.

The problems facing any Egyptian government are many. Agriculture has deteriorated as a result of rising subsoil water, a byproduct of the High Dam and the lack of a drainage system to compensate for the rising water. As the High Dam does not allow silt to pass through, the land requires an extensive use of fertilizers to replace the silt. The average fallah cannot afford to buy fertilizers, so the harvest diminishes in quality and quantity. The other consequence of the loss of silt is that it used to shore up the delta against the encroachment of Mediterranean waters, which are now eroding the delta. Moreover the fish, which gathered at the mouth of the delta to feed on the silt, have disappeared, bankrupting the fish industry. On the other hand, the High Dam and Lake Nasser breed a multiplicity of fish which would be able to supply Egypt with its protein requirements, if fishing and canning industries were set up, which has not been done. Round the lake a whole new system of agriculture could arise, because of the subtropical climate that has been created through evaporation, but that would necessitate a great deal of investment, which has not yet been forthcoming. The major archaeological sites have all been badly damaged as a consequence of increased moisture which destroys the stone. The one advantage of the High Dam to date, and a not inconsequential one, has been that it has saved Egypt from the drought that affected the Sudan.

Because of overpopulation and the decline of agriculture, there has been a progressive depopulation of the countryside and an increasing urbanization. Thus cities and towns grow in size and encroach further onto agricultural land, while reclamation projects cannot keep pace with the amount of agricultural land that is lost every year. Rural inhabitants are lured to the cities by rumours of jobs in factories, in construction work or, even better, by jobs abroad in an oil-rich country at ten times the wages that they can earn at home. Lack of manpower in the countryside has led to the phenomenon of women working in the fields instead of men, and of men seeking work elsewhere and sending money home. While these remittances undoubtedly helped the economy, that venue has eventually diminished as Arab countries have opted to use cheaper Asian labour than the Egyptians who might also sow ideas unpopular with the local rulers. A similar problem is faced by the army. At the moment young Egyptians are employed because they are drafted into the army either on reaching their majority or upon graduating from university. Should the army recruits be demobilized there would be no jobs for them. Unemployment has been endemic for decades. Poverty allied to unemployment is an explosive situation. Over one million babies are born every eight months, yet so long as there is no social security, no old age pension and no medical insurance, Egyptians will continue to produce more and more babies as a means of making their old age secure by being supported by at least one of their children.

The open-door policy and favourable investment terms have attracted, fairly recently, some industries to Egypt, and the government has seemed to rely on the West for financial assistance for industrialization. A confirmation of this policy would lead to dependence on the West for capital. One study of political economy pointed out that dependence on the West might well lead to prosperity, and not necessarily to impoverishment as many economists believe. At the same time the study wondered whether the consequence of the open-door policy might not be labour militancy and the end to Egypt's prized social peace. Labour unions are still government-dominated and do little for the worker in terms of salary negotiations or better working conditions. There are signs of rising labour consciousness, which might well lead to militancy as it has everywhere else. Furthermore an open-door policy does little to protect native industries which are unable to compete with foreign imports which flood the market. The importers prefer to import luxury or consumer items as they stand to make a larger profit on their sales – which raises the question of how long the country can sustain such a high level of consumerism without increasing its level of production. Finally the study wondered what the consequences of an increase in the level of foreign investment would be, when the earnings on investment are repatriated. For preferential terms have been legislated to attract foreign investment, with the result that eventual earnings will have to leave the country. Will the multinational corporations, in alliance with a compradorial class, come to dominate the government as they have done in a number of Third World countries? Will the country become more impoverished in the future? These may not be new problems in the world, for they were faced in the nineteenth century and solved by emigration and colonization of territories, by an agricultural revolution producing higher crop yields and an industrial revolution. Can the same be duplicated today?

These are indeed serious economic issues to ponder, but they are not the only ones. Apart from economic issues, there is the question of Egypt's relations with Israel and with the rest of the Arab world. Sadat had severed relations with the Arab states when both they and he resorted to personal invective after the Camp David accords. Egypt, without the support of the other Arab states, is a small, overpopulated and poor country. Egypt at the head of the Arab world is a power to contend with, both strategically and militarily. Likewise the Arab world without Egypt lacks leadership and political clout. Throughout history Egypt has needed the Arab countries as a natural market and a normal hinterland, a market which used to buy 80 per cent of Egyptian production. That market has been lost. Egypt needs the Arab world as a safety valve for her excess population and the Arab world needs Egyptian expertise in a number of fields, if only to man all the schools from Algeria to the Gulf states with teachers of Arabic, doctors and other professionals. Egypt needs Arab money to be invested, and the Arab countries which once needed Egypt's large army to fight Israel, can no longer use it because of the peace treaty between both countries.

Husni Mubarak, (1981–the present), who succeeded Sadat as president of Egypt, had been named vice-president of the republic by

Sadat and groomed to become his successor. An air force officer with a reputation for efficiency and integrity, Mubarak had been chosen by Nasser to rebuild the Egyptian air force after it had been decimated in 1967. Since he was not identified with any of the power factions that operated under Nasser and during Sadat's early advent to power, Mubarak was chosen by Sadat to become part of his entourage to make sure the air force was controlled by the government, as were the army and the police. Mubarak's efficiency and his no-nonsense attitude to work soon became apparent, and he became invaluable as a negotiator with the Arab countries, who liked his style and respected his low-key attitude. Because of that very style, Sadat had chosen Mubarak as his vice-president as a foil to his own flamboyant personality. The rest of the country assumed that Mubarak would eventually succeed Sadat, unless someone unknown appeared in the wings.

The Mubarak regime faced a tough situation. The economic situation was difficult, but it was not impossible, and the regime was trying to straighten out the economy and repair the abuses of a too-open-door policy by limiting the import of too many consumer articles and balancing the trade figures. It was also trying to encourage productive investments that would improve the economy in the long run and supply employment. The obvious step a government can take to raise capital is to tax its richer citizens, but for the time being the only groups which are successfully taxed are the bureaucrats, who are underpaid to begin with. More stringent methods of taxation of the new rich might alienate the bourgeoisie, and risk scaring foreign capital as well. Much of the foreign capital in Egypt is supplied through banks which have mushroomed in the last decade. Some of these banks are called 'off-shore banks' and are not subject to Egyptian currency regulations, and this poses a potential threat to the economic well-being of the country.

The wheels of any bureaucracy are slow and the Egyptian one is particularly slow since new laws are not quite understood, even by those who have enacted them, so the country teeters between an attempt to impose a free market and an attempt to hold on to part of the public sector which favours the poor. A shot in the arm was supplied when Egypt participated in the Gulf War and a military debt to the United States of some $4.5 billion was cancelled, and she was able to refinance some of her loans, which has cut down on the percentage of capital that was expended on paying interest on foreign loans; nonetheless that percentage of interest is still fairly high, hampering industrial and agricultural investment within the country. Egypt's foreign debt lies in the realm of some 30 billion dollars.

Political parties of all persuasions except the religious have been allowed to form since 1984. However the president still chooses the prime minister, and the entire cabinet is responsible to the president, not to parliament. Whenever presidential elections have taken place, Mubarak has been the sole candidate except for the recent fifth election when Ayman Nour opposed him. For the past twenty five years the Mubarak regime has been characterized by a certain amount of inertia. While the press has become more liberal and opposition papers have flourished, voter turnout in the latest elections showed that the population was staying away from the polling booths. That sign of disaffection with the regime, and alienation from it is caused by the economic situation, and a perception that the future is not any brighter and that the government does not really represent them and their needs. Negotiations with the World Bank and the IMF do not affect the man in the street and therefore he dismisses them from his horizon. He only sees the rising cost of living and the paucity of employment for his children. The international situation further alienated many people who could not condone going to war in the Gulf against fellow Muslims in order to help rich Kuwaitis, many of whom were to be found in the luxury hotels of Cairo. Others who had been in Iraq and who had been thrown out of the country by Saddam, who promised to remit their money and never did, were delighted to go in and clobber Saddam. The outcome of the war where Saddam remained in power but Iraq was destroyed changed people's attitudes. They could not see why Iraq had to be devastated in such a radical fashion, and why their government condoned such excesses on the part of the West against an Arab Muslim country. Events in Yugoslavia and Somalia have raised more questions in the minds of the population who wondered at the inertia on the part of the West in preventing the massacre of Bosnian Muslims, the only ones against whom an arms embargo was sustained. This fed suspicions of Western motives towards the Muslim world in general, exacerbated by activist diatribes that the West is inimical to Muslims, the more so when the Western press is filled with headlines about the 'Muslim Peril'. The mass of the population is non-Westernized, their culture and values are rooted in Islam as a religion and a civilization, they do not want to lose their roots or identity by aping the West and its values, but they do want the benefits of Western technology while maintaining their identity and their cultural values and mores.

The basic issue in Egypt is that the channels of communication between the rulers and the ruled are practically nonexistent. The intellectuals, who should have acted as the conduit for communication between the two groups, abdicated their function when they all served the state, perhaps out of fear during the Nasser regime, or out of conviction. At present they are trying to speak out but will the governing elite listen? The only reason for the government to listen is if violence is threatened by some elements of the population. After the earthquake that took place in winter 1992, a public demonstration did take place. This was an outcry of outrage at the little help those who had suffered from the earthquake were getting. The regions most devastated were in the popular quarters where housing is overcrowded and buildings rarely follow official guidelines, and hence were badly built or so old that the first tremor brought them down. Since Egypt has seldom seen earthquakes in recent memory, the government was slow to react, then made promises of immediate housing which were not forthcoming or which were in farflung areas. The population thus manifested its contempt for these promises, and formed a massive public demonstration. Memories of popular demonstrations remind governments of the events of 1977 when Sadat was forced to call on the army to stop the rampaging crowds from causing further damage in Cairo. Meanwhile fundamentalist groups were in the forefront offering aid and succour to the needy, thereby expanding their popularity among the masses. With rising activist Muslim groups the government has to differentiate between a genuine popular demonstration and one that is led by agents provocateurs, who hope to overwhelm the government security forces.

By then Fundamentalist Islam swept the country, most prominently seen among its women. Larger numbers of 'Muslim' garbed women were seen in the streets coming from all classes of society, yet women were now employed more frequently than ever. The seeming anomaly of modest dress and covered hair on a woman who was a cabinet minister or the vice-president of a bank was simply explained by the fact that the person in question was showing that she is a devout Muslim by her dress. There are many reasons as to why women opted for what they call a 'Muslim' style of clothing, some economic, some social, but mostly to make a statement that they were returning to their social and religious roots and were eschewing the trappings of Westernization but not those of modernization. Thus women use modern tools but eschew Western clothes. Women have become more forceful in recent years, and now there are groups of women interpreting the Koran, previously a male domain, and attempting to establish equality with men not only in the work place. One of the results has been a recent law that allowed women to sue for divorce. However the conditions attached to that suit are a forfeiture of all her legal financial rights. In the eighteenth century women could sue for divorce on the basis of 'darar', that is of damage to herself should the marriage not be voided. In fact the judge had no right to refuse a divorce then. It would seem that the modern era was more stringent towards women's marital rights, continuing to treat women as property of the husband, a notion introduced in the nineteenth century. However women successfully stand for parliament and there are several cabinet ministers in key ministries, and women successfully run large enterprises such as textile mills.

When globalization became the basis for economic activity it was viewed differently by different groups. The artisanal-cum-worker classes viewed it as a bane because they cannot compete with cheaper imported goods, unless they find work in factories. Some factories preferred to hire women because they have no unions and can be hired at cheaper wages and have less protection. Though labour unions are not very powerful they do supply some sort of protection to male workers, but they refuse to include females, seeing them as competition. The middle classes enjoyed having cheaper imported goods. The classes in favour of globalization were those of the compradors and the many emtrepreneurs who produced goods for export. There is a growing degree of economic well-being, money is being made among a new class of entrepreneurs, indeed the stock market, closed since Nasser, is now thriving. Some credit the new economic well-being to the influence of Gamal Mubarak, who is a business man, in changing some laws, thus favouring the private sector. However very few would accept his succession to his father as president. That is a rumour that is constantly bruited in Cairo. Mubarak has not named a successor after 25 years in power and people mutter about hereditary presidencies à la Syria. That will be a hard nut to crack later on. An even harder nut is the result of the growing gap between the rich and the poor.

Signs of wealth are springing up in Egypt with a class of young entrepreneurs, who have created companies and factories that produce a multiplicity of goods and not only for export. Many, like the Sawiris family, have successfully extended their investments outside Egypt. A new affluent class is flaunting its wealth with conspicuous consumption, and the trappings of new millionaires, while the majority of the country is living at or even below the poverty line. That is one of the basic reasons for the rise of fundamentalist Islam, and the notion that only God will provide, since no one else in the country will do so. It has also been partially responsible for the rise of terrorism.

Though political parties have come into existence, save for the religious ones, the only one that has clout is the one that supports the president, the National Democratic Party; the rest have little teeth to them. Parliament is in fact a grouping of yes-men. When an academic, Saad Al-Din Ibrahim made a documentary which mentioned fraudulent returns in a past election he was accused of 'defamation' and imprisoned. He was eventually released from jail through the influence of the Western world, especially the United States. Yet many agreed with him that elections were fraudulent, which partially explains why barely half the population bother to cast a vote. Inertia and cynicism seem to be the twin banes of political life; they can only be lifted if and when a new ideology or a new individual brings in new ideas. In the interim the return to religion and depending on the Almighty to change things is the name of the game. When the United States urged Mubarak to carry out reforms, he amended Article 76 of the constitution which allowed another candidate, Ayman Nour, to stand for president along with Mubarak. Throughout his fourth term Mubarak hinted that he would not stand for a fifth term but then changed his mind and did. He also eased pressure on the press and on the opposition parties, allowing them some teeth. Once the election was over and Mubarak won, he threw Ayman Nour in jail on a charge of falsifying election returns and clamped down on press and parties. He has also extended the emergency law, which had been established in 1981 after Sadat's assassination, for another two years. The government at present is trying to intimidate politicians and judges, who appealed for independence of the judiciary. Once again promised reforms were negated and repression reinstalled. It is no wonder that the man in the street is a confirmed cynic.

Terrorism in Egypt has gone through different stages. At first in 1992 and until 1997 it was aimed at foreigners. Terrorists attacked tourists because they brought money into the country, and that helped the government. They believed that scaring tourists away would bankrupt the government and cause change. That is of course the logic of the anarchists. Later on, in 1993 the terrorists attacked the government directly attempting to assassinate cabinet ministers. Persecution of fundamentalist groupings by the government and widespread arrests and imprisonment of some 20,000 suspects eventually brought these attempts to an end, especially when one of the major groups in 1999 announced that it would no longer resort to violence. In 2000 tourism brought in some $4 billion. Further crackdowns were carried out and for a couple of years no further acts occurred. Acts of terror in the Red Sea area in 2004 and 2005 were aimed at Israeli tourists, although other nationalities were killed as well. The most recent act in 2006 killed many more Egyptians than tourists and suspicion was raised that they were the acts of foreign elements easily infiltrating into the Sinai. However it is difficult to know who is behind these acts, although some bedouin have been arrested. The logic behind these recent acts of terror is one that seems self-defeating because they hurt the average Egyptian who earns his livelihood from tourism more, perhaps, than it hurts the government. If the purpose behind such acts was to rouse the population against the government they have not succeeded, and indeed have antagonized a large part of the population.

Egypt is not an easy country to govern; it has many problems, not enough resources and a population that is growing too rapidly and is mostly young. There are no easy solutions. Some believe that corruption which seems to have become endemic in high places lies at the root of the problem, but that is only one of the problems; the main problems are economic, added to inefficiency in government, a need for massive investments in industry, and a more equitable distribution of wealth. There is also need for a new ideology that can capture the imagination of the young and induce them to set aside their alienation from their government, i.e. a need for a greater degree of liberalization and a government that is clearly seen to represent all sections of society, not only the most affluent. All of this will need time and effort, but the Egyptians are resilient; any country that can cope with a population increase of over 20 million within a decade and not crack at the seams proves that. Time will show whether governments can learn to become more responsible and responsive, and whether the population will work within the system rather than resort to violence and seek to work without.

It is too soon to discover the direction the fifth presidential term in 2005 will take, but there seems to be a cynical outlook among the population that nothing much more different will emerge. Unless a liberal regime is restored, one where the cabinet is responsible to a popularly elected parliament through real, honest elections, and where corruption is rooted out and inefficiency – the result of indifference and loss of hope – is replaced, then the opposition will grow stronger and more militant.

Select bibliography

CHAPTER I

The major reference works dealing with the 7th–13th centuries in Egypt are those written by the Arab chroniclers, or by chroniclers who wrote in Arabic. These are ibn al-Athir, al-Masudi, al-Tabari, Suyuti, and for the later period ibn Taghribirdi and al-Maqrizi. With very few exceptions these works have not been translated into English (except for ibn Taghribirdi) but are referred to in most of the works cited below. Fazlur Rahman, *Islam* (Anchor, 1968) supplies the reader with a basic knowledge of Islam as a religion, while Philip Hitti, A *History of the Arabs* (Macmillan, 1946) gives a chronological account of the Arab expansion until the Abbassi dynasty. J. B. Glubb, *The Great Arab Conquests* (Hodder and Stoughton, 1963) and Gaston Wiet, *L'Egypte arabe* (Paris, 1937) give accounts of the same conquests, the former with a greater emphasis on the military aspects and the latter on the artistic and architectural ones. J. J. Saunders, A *History of Medieval Islam* (Routledge, Kegan Paul, 1965) is a concise and analytic account of the same period which is specially designed for the student of the period, but would do as well for the general reader, while Marshall Hodgson's admirable *The Venture of Islam* (Chicago, 1974) in 3 volumes gives a holistic interpretation of the entire history of the Arab and Muslim worlds. This last work is only to be tackled by the most intrepid scholars for it presents a new vocabulary that has left freshmen weeping, and is only appreciated by specialists in the field. This is not to discourage potential readers, for it is the best work available; it is merely to point out the pitfalls. There are few works on the Tuluni period, one of them being Eustace K. Corbet, 'Life and Works of Ahmad ibn Tulun', in the *Journal of the Royal Asiatic Society* (1891), pp. 527–62. Z. M. Hassan, *Les Tulunides* (Paris, 1933) is a more extensive treatment of the dynasty in French. W. Ivanow, *The Fatimids* (Cambridge, 1940) adequately covers the history of that dynasty as does de Lacy O'Leary, A *Short History of the Fatimid Khalifate* (Dutton, 1928). Stanley Lane-Poole, A *History of Egypt in the Middle Ages* (Methuen, 1901) still remains a standard work since it is largely derived from the works of the chroniclers, although some of his translations are questionable. The era of Saladin and the Crusades has given rise to some brilliant studies among which are S. Runciman, A *History of the Crusades* (Cambridge, 1951–4) in 3 volumes, Kenneth Setton (ed.), A *History of the Crusades* (University of Wisconsin, 1955–7) in 4 volumes, A. Ehrenkreutz, *Saladin* (State University of New York, 1972), and finally Stephen Humphreys, *From Saladin to the Mongols* (State University of New York, 1983).

CHAPTER 2

This period is covered in the chronicles of al-Safawi and al-Suyuti translated by Philip Hitti as *Who's Who in the Fifteenth Century* (New York, 1927), and those of ibn Taghribirdi translated by W. Popper (Berkeley, 1915–60), although not all the volumes were translated. David Ayalon, one of the leading historians of the period, has written *Studies on the Mamluks of Egypt: 125–1517* (Variorum Reprints, 1977) and *Gunpowder and Firearms in the Mamluk Kingdom* (Cass, 1978). An excellent study of urban society which is mostly concentrated on Syria but tells us much about mamluk society is Ira Lapidus, *Muslim Cities in the Later Middle Ages* (Harvard, 1967). Michael Dols, *The Black Death in the Middle East* (Princeton, 1977) describes the plagues that visited Egypt and other areas of the region and their devastating effect on the population and the economy. J. B. Glubb, *Soldiers of Fortune: The Story of the Mamluks* (Stein and Day, 1973) is well worth reading.

CHAPTER 3

P. M. Holt, *Egypt and the Fertile Crescent* (Longmans, 1966) gives a brief narrative of the Ottoman conquest of Egypt and takes the reader up to 1922 and the rise of the modern period. Ibn Iyas, *An Account of the Ottoman Conquest of Egypt* (trans. Royal Asiatic Society, 1921) gives a more detailed picture of the early events. The history of the later mamluks is covered in Shafik Ghorbal, *The Beginnings of the Egyptian Question and the Rise of Mehemet Ali* (Routledge, 1928). Stanford Shaw, *Ottoman Egypt in the Age of the French Revolution* (Harvard, 1964) is an annotated translation of Huseyn Effendi's treatise on Egyptian administration under the mamluks, while Andre Raymond's seminal work *Artisans et commerçants au Caire au 18ème siècle* (Damas, 1973–4) in 2 volumes is a must for the economic history of that period, Afaf Lutfi al-Sayyid's work, *Women and Men in 18th century Egypt* (University of Texas, 1995) is a study of social classes, Nelly Hanna, *In Praise of Books* (Syracuse, 2003) is a cultural history of the middle class in Cairo.

CHAPTER 4

W. E. Lane, *An Account of the Manners and Customs of the Modern Egyptians* (Nattali, 1949) is an enlightening and entertaining social description. Henry Dodwell, *The Founder of Modern Egypt* (Cambridge, 1931) is a cross between a history and a biography of Muhammad Ali. Helen Rivlin, *The Agricultural Policies of Muhammad Ali* (Harvard, 1960) covers much more than the title would lead one to suppose. A revisionist work is Afaf Lutfi al-Sayyid Marsot, *Egypt in the Reign of Muhammad Ali* (Cambridge, 1984). General histories of the century are given in John Richmond, *Egypt 1798–1952* (Columbia, 1977), a knowledgeable and perceptive book, Afaf Lutfi al-Sayyid Marsot, *Egypt and Cromer* (Murray, 1967), A. Goldschmidt, *A Concise History of the Middle East* (Westview, 1979) and John Marlowe, *World Ditch: The Making of the Suez Canal* (Macmillan, 1964) and *Anglo-Egyptian Relations: 1800–1956* (Archon, 1965), F. H. Lawson, *The Social Origins of Egyptian Expansionism during the Muhammad Ali Period* (Columbia: 1992), K. M. Cuno, *The Pasha's Peasants* (Cambridge: 1992) are also revisionist studies of the era.

CHAPTER 5

Afaf Lutfi al-Sayyid Marsot, *Egypt's Liberal Experiment* (University of California, 1977) views the period from the standpoint of the Egyptians. Jacques Berque, *Imperialism and Revolution* (trans. Faber, 1972) is a monumental social history of wide scope that also covers the Nasser years. P. J. Vatikiotis, *A History of Egypt from Muhammad Ali to Sadat* (Johns Hopkins, 1980) is an update of an older work that is especially good on the forties and fifties. Peter Mansfield, *The British in Egypt* (Holt, Rinehart, and Winston, 1972) is a well-written history, while Richard Mitchell, *The Society of the Muslim Brothers* (Oxford, 1969) is the best book on the subject, Malak Badrawi, *Political Violence in Egypt: 1910–1925* discusses early terrorism.

CHAPTER 6

Tom Little, *Modern Egypt* (Praeger, 1967), Peter Mansfield, *Nasser's Egypt* (2nd edn, Penguin, 1969) and John Waterbury, *Egypt: Burdens of the Past, Options for the Future* (University of Indiana, 1978) are general histories of the era. Michael Hudson, *Arab Politics: The Search for Legitimacy* (Yale, 1977) is perhaps the best analysis of the comparative politics of the entire region. Malcolm Kerr, *The Arab Cold War: Gamal Abd al-Nasir and his Rivals, 1958–70* (3rd edn, Oxford, 1971) is an excellent study of inter-Arab rivalries and animosities. William Quandt, *Decade of Decisions: American Policy towards the Arab–Israeli Conflict: 1967–76* (University of California, 1977) details the American attitudes in a lucid fashion as befits someone who was involved in the decision-making process as a senior adviser to Brzezinski, a member of the National Security Council. Robert Mabro, *The Egyptian Economy: 1952–72* (Oxford, 1974) gives an economist's view of the period, while Mark Cooper, *The Transformation of Egypt* (Croom Helm, 1982) and John Waterbury, *The Egypt of Nasser and Sadat* (Princeton, 1983) both give comparative economic history accounts of the two eras. A. I.

Dawisha, *Egypt in the Arab World:* 1952–70 (Halsted, 1977) is also worth reading.

CHAPTER 7

Both the Cooper and Waterbury books previously cited are admirable sources for the seventies, while M. Kerr and S. Yassin (eds.), *Rich and Poor States in the Middle East* (Westview, 1982) is a most felicitous compilation of brilliant analyses and thought-provoking articles by leading local and Western scholars, Amira al-Azhary Sonbol, *The New Mamluks* (Syracuse: 2000) a thought provoking study; Saad el Shazly, *The Crossing of the Suez* (American Mideast Research: 1980) a military memoir; R. A. Hinnebusch Jr, *Egyptian Politics Under Sadat* (Cambridge: 1985); Mohamed Heikal, *The Road to Ramadan* (Collins: 1975); Mohamed Heikal, *Autumn of Fury* (Andre Deutsch: 1983) covers the life and death of Sadat.

The reader might also wish to consult the *Encyclopedia of Islam* as well as the *Middle East Journal* and the *International Journal of Middle East Studies.*

Index